THE ISLANDS SERIES

THE SOLOMON ISLANDS

THE ISLANDS SERIES

The Isle of Arran
*Corsica
*The Falkland Islands
*Grand Bahama
†Harris and Lewis
Lundy
†The Isle of Mull
The Maltese Islands
†Orkney
St Kilda and other Hebridean Outliers
*The Seychelles
†Shetland
*Singapore
*The Solomon Islands
*Vancouver Island

in preparation

The Aran Islands
The Canary Islands: Fuerteventura
Cyprus
Dominica
Puerto Rico
Skye
and many others

* Published in the United States by Stackpole
† Published in the United States by David & Charles

THE
SOLOMON
ISLANDS

by JANET KENT

DAVID & CHARLES : NEWTON ABBOT

STACKPOLE BOOKS : HARRISBURG

To
Peter Orudiana of Malaita, Markson Koroa of Tikopia
and Roy Kelosi of Mono—guides and friends

Set in eleven on thirteen point Baskerville
and printed in Great Britain
by Clarke Doble & Brendon Limited Plymouth

CONTENTS

56577

ILLUSTRATIONS

6

ILLUSTRATIONS

All photographs are by Ted Marriott, Honiara, except where other credits are given

MAPS

Both Maps (Crown copyright)

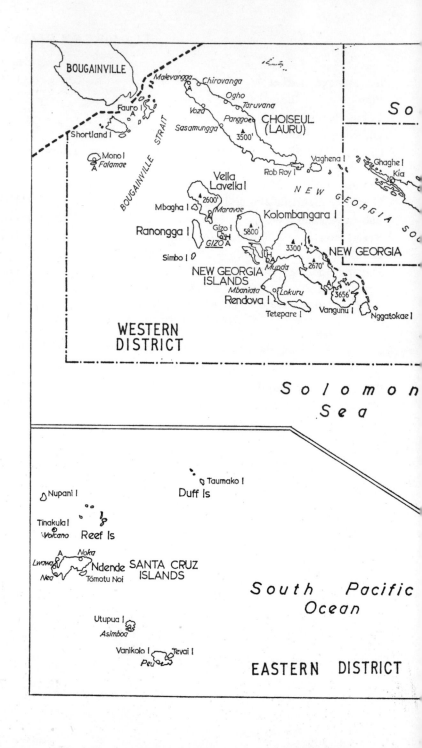

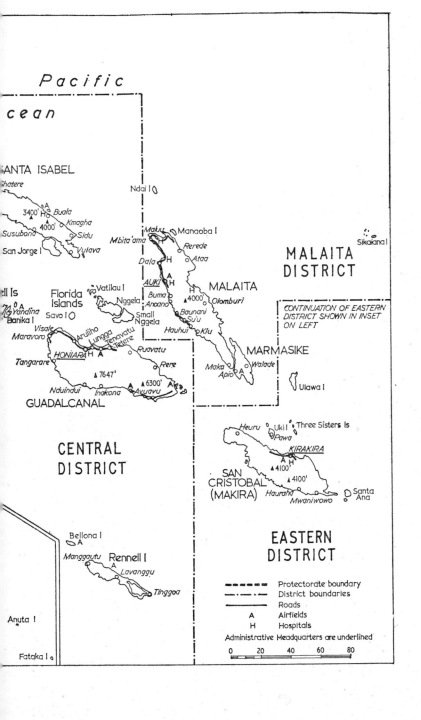

Pacific

cean

SANTA ISABEL

Ghatere

3400' H A Buala
4000' Kmagha
Susubona Sidu
San Jorge I Vulava

ll Is
Florida
Yandina Islands
Banika I Savo I O

Visale
Maravoro
Aruligo
Tangarare
HONIARA H A
▲7647'
Nduindui Inakona
GUADALCANAL

Ndai I O

Maluu Manaoba I
Mbita'ama Rerede
Dala H Ataa
AUKI H
A
Buma H
Anoano ▲4000' Olomburi
Nggela Baunani
Small Su'u
Nggela
Hauhui Klu

Vatilau I

Tenavatu
Lungga Tetere
Puavatu
Rene
▲6300'
▲ Avuavu A

MALAITA

MARMASIKE

Maka Walade
Apio A

Sikaiana I

MALAITA
DISTRICT

CONTINUATION OF EASTERN
DISTRICT SHOWN IN INSET
ON LEFT

Ulawa I

CENTRAL
DISTRICT

Heuru Uki I Three Sisters Is
Pawa
KIRAKIRA
A H
SAN ▲4100'
CRISTOBAL ▲4100'
(MAKIRA) Haurahá Santa
Mwaniwowo Ana

Bellona I
A
Manggautu Rennell I
A
Lavanggu

Tinggoa

Anuta I

Fataka I

EASTERN
DISTRICT

- - - - - Protectorate boundary
- · - · - District boundaries
———— Roads
A Airfields
H Hospitals
Administrative Headquarters are underlined

0   20   40   60   80

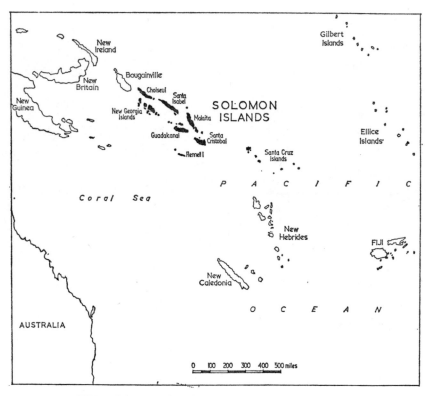

THE SOLOMON ISLANDS IN RELATION
TO AUSTRALIA

1 MOUNTAINOUS GREEN ISLANDS

FROM the air the first impression of the Solomons is one of colour, of mountainous green islands sprawling against the shifting blue of the sea. Sandy beaches disappear among a confusion of palm trees. Canoes scud gently across tranquil bays, protected from the white-capped waves by coral reefs. Within the reefs are some of the last unspoiled and virtually unknown areas of the world.

Visitors flying in from Fiji or Papua–New Guinea, the main countries to provide a direct service to the Solomons, land at Honiara airport, nine miles east of the small and pleasant capital of the same name, and the only town in the island group. Honiara is situated on the north coast of Guadalcanal, the largest island in the Solomons, and in 1942 the scene of one of the bloodiest campaigns of the Pacific war. More than 30,000 Japanese and American troops died in its jungles. Much of the fighting took place on the Guadalcanal plain, around the site of the present airport, then a hotly-disputed landing strip, and today a renovated artillery piece, the sole reminder of the war, stands rather incongruously outside the main entrance. The airport is small and compact; incoming aircraft taxi practically to the door of the single-storey main building, which is just as well in the hot and humid climate. Inside the building customs officials in their red berets, blue shirts and dark shorts and the occasional policeman in his peaked cap, blue shirt and khaki shorts deal with the formalities quickly and, usually, efficiently. A noticeable feature is the lack

11

of white faces among the airport officials. Localisation of government posts has not been rapid in the Solomons but customs and police are two departments which have a good record in this respect.

Outside the airport a special bus takes arrivals to Honiara. The trip into the town must be one of the most attractive journeys from any airport in the world. The road lies parallel to the beach, with the sea on one side and on the other thickly wooded mountains at the edge of the plain. Nearer to the capital one or two buildings are passed—a small tobacco factory, a workshop, a biscuit factory, the government secondary school in its grounds—and a small fishing village, whose occupants moved themselves bodily from another island in the group to establish a new home on Guadalcanal. On the outskirts of the town buildings grow more frequent : the concrete dormitories of the labour lines where the unmarried labourers live, and above them, on the ridges, the larger and more spacious houses of government officials. Flamboyant trees line the road, their foliage a riot of red. Then over the Matanikau river by a narrow, single-traffic bridge and into Honiara itself, journey's end for many tourists but only a tiny and unrepresentative part of the Solomon Islands.

PREVIEW OF THE PROTECTORATE

The Solomons are beautiful. The white sands, coral reefs and placid lagoons present an idyllic picture, and the artificial islands of Malaita, the crater lake of Tikopia and the rugged grandeur of the hinterland of Guadalcanal offer spectacles that few other countries can equal. There are drawbacks, of course. In this humid climate Europeans usually find it impossible to walk for more than a hundred yards without breaking into a sweat. Storms can be rough and dangerous. It often rains for hours or even days at a time in the wet season. There are few amenities for the sophisticated visitor. On the other hand, where else in the world today can the visitor see so many age-old customs so long preserved almost unchanged? The bride-price ceremonies of Malaita, the manufacture of red feather money on Santa Cruz and the talking drums of San Cristobal are only a few of the many island traditions which have been maintained over the centuries.

The people of the Solomons are genuinely friendly and courteous. Anyone who visits the islands is sure of a warm welcome, especially if he is willing to leave the main tourist routes—such as they are. Getting to the islands in the first place is not easy, but three flights a week from Port Moresby link with connecting services from Australia to Papua–New Guinea, while three more flights a week bring passengers in from Nadi in Fiji, via the New Hebrides. Connecting flights link Fiji with Hawaii, the west coast of the United States and Australia.

The Solomons, hundreds of them—the total has never been estimated—extend for some 900 miles in a south-easterly chain from Papua–New Guinea across the Coral Sea about 1,200 miles north-east of Australia. There are ten main clusters which are all inhabited, except for a few barren atolls. These islands range in size from tiny reefs a few feet in diameter to Guadalcanal, the largest island 90 miles long and 30 wide, with mountains up to 8,000ft. The other large islands are Malaita, San Cristobal, Santa Isabel, Choiseul and New Georgia. They share the same general topography, all of them mountainous, covered with thick tropical rain forests and intersected by rivers. But there is little else uniform about the Solomons. Diversity is the keynote. From Australian-administered Bougainville and Buka in the west, right down the double chain of islands to the Santa Cruz group and beyond in the east, there is enormous variety in almost every feature—in geology, ethnology, customs, language, natural history, and so on.

Bougainville and Buka apart, the Solomon group, with its total land mass of 11,500 square miles and 161,000 inhabitants, forms the British Solomon Islands Protectorate and is administered from Honiara by the High Commissioner for the Western Pacific

13

who is appointed from London. This protectorate has been divided into four districts: western district, with its administrative centre at Gizo; central district which includes Honiara, the capital; Malaita, with its district station at Auki; and eastern district, which has its headquarters at Kirakira. About 400 expatriate officials, accompanied by their families and mainly British but with a sprinkling of Australians, Fijians and New Zealanders, assist with the administration of government and the running of the various departments. For many years the government could be described as a benevolent paternalism operating on a shoestring budget, aided by the soporific climate, distance from London and general lack of interest displayed by Whitehall. Lately, however, encouraged by a growing internal demand for independence, there have been great changes.

Even so, the vast majority of Melanesians, Polynesians and Micronesians living outside the capital and district stations have little contact with the government and not much idea of what is going on. Most of them live as their ancestors have lived for generations, dwelling in small villages, isolated from the outside world. They engage in a little subsistence farming and sea fishing, and perhaps grow some copra as a cash crop. It is a pleasant and fairly unexacting way of life. The average islander has only to work in his gardens for one or two days a week in order to support his family, which leaves the rest of the time for fishing, pig hunting, storytelling and just 'going walkabout'.

In the almost perpetual sun few clothes are needed; for the men a lap lap or a pair of shorts is sufficient, while the women in the villages usually wear only a skirt or perhaps a cotton dress. Housing is no problem; homes of leaf and bamboo can be erected in a comparatively short time. Money is necessary only for such luxuries as tobacco, beer, kerosene, tinned meat—and for paying taxes. This money—Australian dollars are the legal tender—may be obtained from the sale of copra and market produce, or by the younger men hiring themselves out as plantation labourers. However, with the improving standard of education some children who have got as far as two years at a secondary school can get jobs in government service, usually in Honiara. This of course entails an almost permanent break with village life, which the young people often welcome but which causes concern among the older folk.

The Solomon Islands form part of the chain of Melanesian islands on the eastern fringe of the large archipelago of the East Indies, but include also a number of Polynesian outliers. The term Melanesia means dark islands, from the Greek *melas*, black, and *nesia*, islands. This name is probably derived either from the lowering storm clouds sometimes seen over the islands or from the effect of the dark vegetation on the hillsides, and not from the colour of the skins of their inhabitants.

The typical island has a flat coastal belt bearing coconut palms and where rivers run out to the sea there may well be swamps and dense growths of mangrove and ivory-nut trees. The rolling foothills beyond are covered in kumai grass, scrub and fern, with some scattered trees, and the greater part of the interior consists of forested hills and mountain ranges, steepening as the centre is approached.

The off-shore reefs sometimes form lagoons, some more than thirty miles long and containing small islands. Harbours and anchorages are generally good, with the exception of the south coast of Guadalcanal and part of San Cristobal which are both poorly served in this respect.

The most prominent aspects of the geological formation of the Solomons are the sometimes spectacular coral atolls and raised coral reefs. Volcanic activity, however, seems to have played a large part, and the core of the main islands is composed of ancient lavas overlaid with sedimentary and volcanic material of later date. P. J. Coleman has divided the Solomons into five geological sub-regions or provinces. The central province, including Choiseul, Guadalcanal, the Floridas and south-west Santa Isabel is noted

for its exposures of Pre-Tertiary igneous and metamorphic base-
ment complex which have been shaped and altered by faulting.
The volcanic rocks of Guadalcanal are Pre-Miocene. In the
Pacific province, which includes Malaita, Ulawa and north-east
Santa Isabel, we have basaltic lavas covered with sediments that
are essentially pelagic with a small terrigenous content. The island
of Ulawa is rimmed with a twenty-foot terrace of Quaternary
reef limestone. The volcanic province embraces the Shortlands,
the New Georgia group, the Russells and Savo, a quiescent volcano which has erupted several times in the last few hundred years,
but not since 1840. There are at least thirty-four recognisable
volcanic centres in the Solomons but though volcanic activity
still occurs it is not usually severe, and earthquakes, while quite
frequent, are not usually of great magnitude.

In addition to Savo, Simbo in the west is active and so is a
submarine volcano in the New Georgia group. These volcanoes are
spread over a belt 350 miles long and about 50 miles wide, some
in Coleman's volcanic province and some in his oceanic volcanic
province which consists of the Santa Cruz group and a number
of isolated volcanic islands in the eastern district. Tinakula
(3,000ft) in the Santa Cruz group is active; in 1971 occupants
of the island had to be evacuated after an eruption. Tikopia, a
Polynesian island in this group, is a fine example of a volcano
which has breached and blown away its cone by paroxysmal
eruption. The fifth sub-region, the atoll province, comprises the
outlying atolls around the Solomons, among them Ontong Java,
Roncador Reef, the Reefs, Rennell and Bellona. Parts of the
atoll of Ontong Java have been stabilised to form vegetated sand
cays a few feet above sea-level. Rennell and Bellona, on the
other hand, are both uplifted atolls.

In recent years there has been a good deal of prospecting for
minerals, fired by the success of similar investigations in Bougainville where considerable deposits of copper have been found and
are now being mined on a large scale. In 1968 an aerogeophysical
project sponsored by the United Nations was completed. Con-

16

siderable deposits of bauxite were revealed on Rennell and copper on Guadalacanal, and commercial prospecting followed on both islands. Prospecting for other minerals continues, in an optimistic spirit, especially on Santa Isabel where deposits of nickel and cobalt are sought, and on Rennell where the possibility of extracting limestones has also been examined. Several commercial oil companies display a cautious interest in looking for off-shore deposits of oil in the Solomon seas. While some officials are convinced that the answer to the Solomons' shaky economy lies in its as-yet-undiscovered mineral wealth, the general attitude to all this prospecting has been of a hopeful but rather sceptical nature, something like that of the owner of a single premium bond awaiting the weekly draw.

THE TWO SEASONS

Temperatures in the Solomons seldom exceed 32° C during the day or fall below 22° C at night. The islands enjoy a tropical oceanic climate, that is to say that although it is hot and humid, the cool winds and abundant rainfall make it quite pleasant to live in, although tending to encourage indolence. The climate has been blamed for the reluctance of islanders to adopt new farming methods, but it has not yet been advanced as an excuse for the failure of some expatriates to show more than a modicum of enthusiasm for their work.

The prevailing winds dictate the two main climatic seasons. The wet season extends from November to April. During this period the weather is uncertain, most of the winds coming from the west or north-west. Long periods of calm are punctuated by squalls, sometimes severe, and occasionally by the build-up of cyclones, which form in the Coral Sea and Solomons area and pass on to the New Hebrides, New Caledonia, Fiji and Australia, increasing in intensity as they go and causing much more damage in these territories than in the Solomons, although now and again the group does suffer. When this happens it can be a matter of weeks or even months before the full extent of the damage in the outer islands is known. In the last twenty years both Tikopia and Ontong Java have been ravaged by hurricanes and it was some time before the rest of the protectorate knew of the plight of these remote areas and could send assistance.

From May to October the south-east trade winds blow almost continuously but with varying intensity. Periods of up to ten days or more of strong winds with gusts of 25–30 knots and rain squalls are followed by fine days with light south-east winds of 5–10 knots. This is the dry season.

Throughout the year the days are hot, but cool land breezes from the mountains usually make the coastal strips pleasantly fresh in the evening; the major islands are high enough to allow the coastal temperatures to fall occasionally as low as 19° C. Rainfall in the interior mountainous areas is heavy at all times, causing streams and rivers to flood in a surprisingly short time. Even when the sun is obscured by rain clouds, however, its rays can still be fierce, and care has to be taken to avoid sunburn in overcast weather as well as at other times.

Average rainfall figures vary from island to island. At Honiara the average is 85in a year, while at Vanikolo in the eastern district it is over 200in. Such is the power of the sun that the effect of the heaviest downpour soon vanishes.

C. H. Allen has pointed out that while all Solomon Islanders recognise the existence of the two main seasons and name them after the local words for the respective winds, they usually define the seasons in terms of their own regular activities and the occurence of natural phenomena. For example, there is the season when the yams are planted, the season when bonito are plentiful in the sea, when turtles are mating and when various crops are harvested.

GROUND COVER

The soils of the Solomons vary from area to area, but there are three main types : from volcanic rocks, from limestone, and from alluvial deposits. There are variations on these three main categories. Some of the volcanic soils, particularly those on Rendova in the west, are extremely fertile. Some soils, however, consist of a top coating of volcanic dust over thin coral with a subsoil of clay. The limestone soil is not very fertile on the plains, where it becames waterlogged easily, but is better on high ground. Most of the island soils are porous so that while it is true that the average Solomon Islander exists by subsistence farming, it cannot be said that the ground in which he has to grow his food is highly fertile.

Solomon Islanders are fond of flowers and both men and women wear them in their hair. The red and yellow flowers of the hibiscus plant are particularly favoured as decorations. There are also many types of orchid growing wild in the islands. At least 230 different specimens are known to grow there, some believed to be peculiar to the group. The most common are *Dendrobium* and *Bulbophgenera*, but by far the most spectacular is *Dendrobium spectabile*, which grows only in the Solomons and neighbouring New Guinea, and *Dendrobium johnsoniae* with its large white flower sometimes 3in across. In coastal areas *Dendrobium gouldii* grows prolifically and is noted for its variety of colours on different islands, a yellow and brown type, for instance, is found on Guadalcanal, white on Malaita and San Cristobal, and mauve on Gela.

In coastal areas free of mangrove swamps, many of the beaches are relatively clear with only a few coconut palms dotted about the shore area; these are conditions liked by the casuarina and such plants as the convolvulus *canavalia*. Where the trees push thickly to the water's edge *Cycas circinalis* grows in large numbers.

More than 90 per cent of the land area of the Solomons is covered with trees. There are two main categories of forest: coastal, subdivided into beach forest and mangrove forest, and primary inland forest, subdivided into lowland and foothill forest, freshwater swamp, and mountain forest. Away from the coastal strips the rain forest becomes increasingly dense, forming an enclosed world of its own with few flowers growing in its sunless interior. Some trees grow to more than 150ft. One of the most distinctive in girth is the banyan. In the coastal areas the most commonly found species is *Securinega samoana*, while around the river banks there often congregate *Spondias dulcis*, *Albizzia salomonensis*, and *Caruga floribunda*. *Caolphyllum kajewskii*, which constituted about 60 per cent of the timber volume worked in the forest area of Gizo island between 1963 and 1968, likes swampy areas near the coast. *Terminalia brassii* and *Metroxylon salomonensis*, or ivory nut, are also found near swamps.

Among the mountain forests of the Solomons *Casuarina nodiflora* is one of the best-known trees; *Dacrydium elatum* is fairly common and *Agathis macrophylla* rather less so. On some ridges trees give way to bramble, *Rubus hasskarlii*, with its long roots reaching to 20 and 30ft. Great stretches of ground are also covered by alang-alang grass and various ferns.

DUGONGS AND MEGAPODES

There are relatively few mammals indigenous to the Solomons. Before the arrivals of the Spaniards in the sixteenth century there were only dogs and pigs among the larger mammals, and wild pigs, with long snouts and sharp back bristles, are still hunted today. Most dogs are domesticated though some have taken to the bush in packs where they roam wild, but they are generally timid and indeed are less aggressive than some of the descendants of domestic cats introduced by Europeans, which took to the jungle and bred there and now live by killing small birds. Solomon Islanders are not sentimental about domestic animals and those dogs and cats maintained in the villages have to work for a living, acting as guards and killing off rats.

The cuscus (*Phalanger orientalis breviceps*), a marsupial varying in colour from white through stages of grey to black, inhabits most of the islands, apart from the Santa Cruz group. Among the several types of rat there are the large tree-dwelling *Cyromys* and

Musrex. The common brown rat is found in large numbers where-
ever there are people, some islanders being practically overrun by
these vermin. Taumako in the Duff Islands suffers particularly
heavily from their depredations. When asked why the people did
not import cats to deal with the rats an elder replied 'We did, but
the rats ate the cats!' One feels that perhaps this islander was
engaging in the traditional pastime of kidding the expatriate.
There are bats, too, particularly the fruit bat commonly known as
the flying fox. During the day these bats sleep together in colonies
in trees, emerging at night. The din of a congregation of flying
foxes has to be heard to be believed, but their chattering is
encouraged by the islanders who stalk them both for food and for
their teeth, which are made into necklaces. In addition to the
flying fox a number of smaller bats lurk nocturnally in the islands;
these are insectivorous and happily number mosquitoes among
their victims.

In 1970 over 11,000 head of cattle were imported by the Department of Agriculture and by private firms. Most of these animals
are being grazed on plantations to help clear the undergrowth
among the trees. Some are for slaughtering, and the beef is of
course sold locally. One or two mission stations have been grazing
cattle successfully for some years but several previous attempts by
the government and commercial concerns to import herds have
come to grief. In a number of cases no sooner had the cattle set
foot on dry land than they bolted into the interior. Today some of
them are roaming wild on Guadalcanal plain to the delight of the
local inhabitants who are not above surreptitiously encouraging
members of the domestic herds to join them.

The water mammals of the Solomons are rather more interesting than the land animals. The dolphins off the coast of Malaita
are the victims of a traditional hunt which has been the subject of
magazine articles and films. As soon as a school of dolphins has
been sighted the islanders gather in their canoes and drive the
mammals towards the beach by banging stones together under
water or by waving shell rattles. The resultant din frightens and

bewilders the dolphins who become separated from each other and are easily caught and killed.

Whales used to be seen quite frequently off the shores of the islands, particularly the finback, sperm and sulphur-belly varieties, but the organised whaling expeditions of the last two centuries drastically depleted the number of whales in the Pacific. Today an occasional whale is beached after a storm and is quickly slaughtered and eaten, but this does not happen often. Dugong are more numerous. The newly calved female of this species possesses a pair of mammary glands which probably gave rise to the belief in the existence of mermaids. Some people of Malaita consider themselves to be descended from the dugong and so are not allowed to hunt or eat these creatures. Two kinds of turtle inhabit the Solomon seas, the green giant leatherbacked variety, and the more common turtle which is hunted for its shell, this sometimes fetching a good price commercially. Land reptiles abound but are usually harmless. Even snakes with venomous bites rarely attack people unless provoked, and give very little trouble. The local Department of Agriculture has been running a campaign to persuade people not to kill snakes as they are instrumental in destroying rats. There are about twenty different species of snakes, and many islanders associate them with ghosts and spirits of their ancestors. This never prevents snakes from being killed, but they are not eaten. Some pagan tribes of the interior of Malaita still worship the snake known locally as *loi*. The Lau people of North Malaita fear the species they call *baekwa i Tolo*. If a man comes across one of these curled up on his path through the bush it is regarded as an omen of death.

The largest snake in the islands is the python; specimens 9ft long have been found in the interior. Two snakes have been named after Europeans. Guppy's snake, named after an amateur geologist who paid a visit to the islands towards the end of the nineteenth century, is of medium size and brown with dark stripes. Its bite can be extremely painful. The other snake resembles the Australian copperhead and was named after Charles Woodford, one of the first Europeans to study wild life in the islands, and the first Resident Commissioner of the Solomons at the close of the nineteenth century.

In Honiara the Pacific boa, a slow-moving brown-coloured nocturnal snake, is sometimes encountered. Other snakes living in the town area are the red-banded tree snake and the whip snake. The former sometimes exceeds 6ft in length; it is red or yellow with a yellow underbelly and lives on rats and birds. The whip snake is blue-grey and seldom more than 3ft long. It can move swiftly and is extremely cautious, rarely being seen. Also to be found is the blind *Typhlops*, very small and worm-like in appearance and completely harmless.

There are many different lizards. The most common is the gecko, small and bold, which occupies houses, attaching himself to the walls or ceiling and living off small insects. There are also several types of skink. Largest of all lizards is the monitor or goanna, sometimes more than 5ft long. This reptile is found more often in the forest than in town, and it has been suggested that it was driven away from Honiara by *Bufo maranus*, introduced into Honiara from the southern states of America. These toads secrete a virulent poison in their glands, potent enough to kill quite a large snake. In addition to the imported toad there are various local species of frog, among them a number of horned and tree frogs and the huge *Rana guppyi* which sometimes weighs over 2lb and is found close to rivers.

Of the larger reptiles pride of place must go to the crocodile. The Australian crocodile (*Crocodilus porosus*) lives both in fresh and salt water. It often swims out to sea from one river mouth and makes its way along the shore, into another river mouth and back into the interior. Islanders have been attacked and killed by crocodiles while hunting them, but as a rule these reptiles confine their diet to fish, cuscus and unwary pigs. As crocodile skins fetch a high price their numbers are being reduced by systematic hunting.

About 150 different species of birds have been identified among the permanent and migratory land and fresh-water birds of the

Solomons, among them the red-throated dabchick of the grebe family and four varieties of heron and bittern. The Australian grey duck is the only one of its species in the islands, but there are a number of hawks and eagles including the crested hawk, the white and red eagle kite, the goshawk, the pied hawk and—the only large one among them—Sandford's eagle. This bird has a wing span of 3ft and is found both on the coast and inland up to a height of 4,000ft. It feeds on pigeons and fish.

Perhaps the most unusual bird in the group is the megapode, which flourishes on Savo and parts of Guadalcanal as well as in the western Solomons. It is smaller than a chicken but lays an egg as big as a turkey's, which it then buries some 2 to 6ft deep in the sand to be hatched by heat from the sun or from adjacent thermal springs. The baby megapode is able to dig itself up out of the sand and run and fly almost at once.

Pigeons and doves abound, there being over twenty species of them in the islands. Less attractive are the hornbills with their ungainly motion and huge bills in which they crack fruit and nuts. At nesting time the female occupies the hollow interior of a tree which the male plasters up with mud, feeding its mate through a tiny aperture until the young are hatched.

About twelve species of kingfisher have been observed. Equally attractive are the parrots, cockatoos and lories. There are a dozen different species of these, including the tiny pigmy parrot and the splendid king parrot. The oriental cuckoo is one of seven species of this family known to visit the Solomons, albeit rarely. Owls too are scarce but some have been seen. Among the song birds are thrushes, swallows, warblers, flycatchers, whistlers and starlings. There has been one report of a number of pelicans landing briefly in the group but these seem never to have returned.

Among the multitude of insects, the most beautiful is the butter-fly in its many varieties, some large enough to be described as 'bird-winged'. Most brightly coloured of all are *Papilio, Troides* and *Ornithoptera* sometimes measuring as much as 10in from wingtip to wingtip. Hawk moths, which feed on flowers while still on the wing and usually only come out at night, are also common; and the many dragonflies, drifting over the streams and rivers of the interior, almost rival the butterflies in colour. Sandflies, centipedes and scorpions are among the less pleasant forms of insect life, and ants, houseflies, spiders, caterpillars and a whole host of other creatures appear in all sorts of shapes and sizes.

Over twenty different species of mosquito have been identified, including the malaria-spreading *Anopheles punctulatus*. A malaria-spraying scheme backed by the World Health Organisation has cleared some of the islands of this mosquito but it still flourishes in others.

At one time it was said that only in the Solomon seas did most fish die of old age. Lately, however, there have been several determined efforts by commercial organisations to organise the large-scale catching of fish which abound in the waters off the islands. There are many sharks, including the hammer-headed variety, and these take a regular toll of lives, making swimming off the beaches a dangerous activity. Barracuda, too, can be extremely dangerous. Crayfish, squid, tuna, kingfish and the sea slug known as bêche-de-mer are all caught, some now on a commercial basis but most from small canoes by men fishing for their families. Crabs are a popular delicacy. Mother-of-pearl shell and trochus shell are exported, although not in large quantities, and there is a small but growing industry in the export of shells to collectors.

2   CLANNISH PEOPLE

A T the 1970 census there were 160,998 people living in the Solomons. Of these 149,667 were Melanesians, 6,399 were Micronesians (Gilbertese), 1,280 were Europeans, 577 were Chinese, and 713 were of mixed descent. There were 85,179 males and 75,819 females. 71,761 boys and girls were fourteen years of age and under. Only 2,122 people were 75 years of age and older.

The most heavily populated area in any island was on Tikopia where two square miles of land were occupied by over 1,000 people. The greatest overall density of population was on Malaita and the two smaller islands of Ontong Java and Sikaiana. Here a population of 51,722, almost a third of the total population of the Solomons, was concentrated over an area of 1,754 square miles to provide an average of 29·49 people per square mile. The most sparsely populated district was the west where a population of 32,231 occupied 3,310 square miles, averaging 9·74 people per square mile. The least heavily populated major island was Santa Isabel with a total of 8,653 people distributed at a density of 5·58 per square mile.

Eleven thousand one hundred and ninety-one people live in Honiara, the capital, and a few thousand more in the district centres of Auki, Gizo and Kirakira. The rest, well over 90 per cent of the population, lived in villages.

When asked where he comes from, the average Solomon Islander names the island of his birth. Few occupants of the group regard themselves as Solomon Islanders; they are Malaita men or Tikopians or Reef Islanders as the case may be. These differences are maintained wherever islanders congregate—in the capital, at boarding schools, plantations and other places of employment. Inter-island rivalries, although less intense than they once were, still exist, and brawls between groups from different districts are not unknown.

The occupants of the western islands have on the whole come closest to adapting to the European way of life. There are a number of reasons for this. In the first place the westerners are a shrewd and adaptable race and they have seen that to get the best out of life they must conform to European standards, because the expatriates at the moment provide both employment and the means of advancement. There are more schools in the western district than in any other part of the Solomons and a higher proportion of students go on to secondary education. Because the westerners had their settlements on the coast, there was immediate contact with Europeans when they first sailed through the islands on their voyages of discovery, and there has been a longer tradition of co-operation with white people than elsewhere in the Solomons where native settlements were inland.

Another reason for the relative smoothness with which the westerners have come to terms with the expatriate culture and civilisation lies in the physical beauty of the women of the district. For over a hundred years European planters, traders and government officers have taken western girls as mistresses and wives. Consequently a large number of half-castes have grown up with a good knowledge of the English language and a willingness and even a desire to lead a European way of life.

Physically westerners are darker than most Melanesians and

27

tend to be taller and slimmer; the men of Roviana, descendants of head-hunters, are the toughest of them.

The occupants of Santa Isabel, the large island almost at the centre of the group, take a great pride in their home. They are the most united of all the island races: the Isabel people were the first to take over the running of their junior primary schools from the missions; they are the only group to have built their own club house in Honiara, and the Isabel Council has launched a number of progressive schemes including a trade-training and rural development school for children who do not achieve a secondary education.

The bulk of the population of Santa Isabel occupies the south-east corner of the island; in the head-hunting days the Roviana men decimated the inhabitants of the north-west. There is a great interest in the island's history and traditions; their dances tend to be more intricate than those of other islands, their ceremonial attire more ornate, and the great war shields of Santa Isabel are beautifully designed works of art. The men are less aggressive than those of some other islands, but this has not prevented them from occupying important posts in government service. Indeed it is perhaps indicative of the character of these people that although many of them were captured and taken into slavery by western islanders, within two generations the descendants of the Santa Isabel slaves had married into their captors' families and in some cases had become headmen. Only the people of Santa Isabel take enough pride in their good name to persuade their young men without work in Honiara to return home so that they do not drift into trouble in the capital.

The Malaita people are, on the whole, disliked and feared by the inhabitants of other islands. 'Those Malaita men are like elephants, they never forget an injury', said one prominent Savo man, and his view is shared by many. There is a grave shortage of arable land on Malaita, which is overcrowded by Solomons standards, and this has led to a tradition of Malaita men leaving home in order to earn a living, especially among the younger sons who do not inherit much land. While the average islander can get enough from his land to ensure him a fairly easy life, the Malaita man has never been in this happy position. Instead he has had to go and work on plantations and in the capital.

More insular and withdrawn than the extroverted western and Polynesian people and clinging more tenaciously to their customs and traditions, Malaitans are often dour and withdrawn. They are also aggressive and quick to anger. Their pride frequently prevents them from coming to terms with the expatriate influence in the Solomons. Malaita men have seldom paid lip-service to alleged European superiority and their insistence on being treated as men and not children has not always endeared them to the more colonially minded among government officials. On the other hand, while distrusting all strangers in general and whites in particular, once a Malaitan gives his friendship to anyone it usually endures. Other islanders, wary of the proud and tough Malaita men, treat them with reserve. They feel that the Malaitans may well decide to take over the whole of the Solomons one day, and this is a cause of some unease.

The people of the eastern Solomons have had less contact with Europeans than most islanders. The islands are scattered and the area has in the past been a distressed one, receiving fewer educational facilities than the other areas. The people of the district on the whole are not very interested in what goes on in the rest of the islands and indeed talk of going up 'to the Solmons' when they want to visit other districts, a sign that they do not regard themselves as part of the main group. There have been indications lately, however, that this district will pay a more prominent part in the affairs of the protectorate, largely due to the efforts of Solomon Mamaloni, an elected member of the governing council from one of the eastern areas. Mamaloni is easily the most enterprising and forthright of the younger politicians.

One island technically in the eastern sector of the protectorate but in reality a law unto itself is Tikopia, a remote Polynesian outlier. This island, like Malaita, is overcrowded and many young

29

Tikopians have left in order to live and work in one of the Tikopian communities that have sprung up in the other islands. The Tikopians are an attractive people with a distinctive culture, and though cheerful, hard-working and extremely strong, they have in the past been regarded as slow-thinking but this is almost certainly due to the inadequate educational facilities with which the island once had to contend. There are many stories about the brawls between the Tikopians and the Malaitans whenever the two groups meet. A prominent battleground was once Lever's plantation on Yandina in the Russell Islands, where Tikopians and Malaitans worked as plantation hands. On one memorable occasion a large number of them lined up to settle things with a 'battle', and though both Malaitans and Tikopians later claimed to have been the victors, it appears that this time the Tikopians had the better of the encounter. The inhabitants of the other Polynesian islands tend to keep more to themselves; indeed for many years special precautions had to be taken over entry to the particularly isolated islands of Rennell and Bellona lest the slightest cold should start a serious epidemic. The Polynesian islands are discussed in more detail on pages 61–4.

The people of Guadalcanal, Savo and the Floridas are sturdy and undemonstrative. During the war they were loyal to the Allied cause and rescued many stranded American airmen and sailors and guided them back to their lines. Although the Guadalcanal coastal areas have plenty of contact with strangers, the men and women of the interior, or bush, remain isolated. The coastal dwellers and bush people get on well enough on this island, but on Malaita even today there is constant rivalry and animosity between the two.

The minority groups in the Solomons consist of Europeans, Fijians, Gilbertese and Chinese. Each group is a fairly tight-knit community with little contact with the local people. A few Europeans live away from the capital and district centres, mainly missionaries and planters, but most of them work for the government in Honiara, and the majority of these seldom leave the capital. The Chinese play a prominent part in the commercial life of the Solomons; there is a Chinatown in Honiara and Chinese-owned stores in the district centres. A number of Chinese merchants own ships which tour the islands buying copra and selling trade goods. Most Solomon Islanders dislike and distrust the Chinese, accusing them of cheating them in the stores and claiming that they make islanders pay more than Europeans.

The Fijians occupy a small section of Honiara and also work in the district centres. For the most part the men work as foremen and skilled mechanics for the public works department. They are regarded as a well-behaved and civic-conscious group, but Fijians have little time for either Solomon Islanders or Europeans, although they are invariably polite. The men regard themselves as physically far superior to all other men in the Solomons, which they are, and are quietly contemptuous of the islanders because they have not yet attained independence. Many islanders would like to see the Fijians replaced by indigenes and there is little doubt that this will happen as soon as there are enough trained Solomon Islanders available.

Gilbertese, resettled from the Gilbert and Ellice Islands in recent years, occupy several communities in the western district and a section of Honiara. They maintain their own traditions and mingle little with Solomon Islanders. They are an extremely intelligent people and this is beginning to become a minor problem in the western area where Gilbertese children are in some cases outshining local children at school, and moving on in increasing numbers to secondary education, which not all Melanesian children are able to secure. Melanesians regard the Gilbertese as scruffy and indolent, accusing them of not keeping up the settlements they have been allocated and of neglecting their plantations. They think the attitude of the British government in transplanting the Gilbertese to the Solomons extremely high-handed. In the last ten years there have been some fifty marriages between Gilbertese and Solomon Islanders and it is hoped that in this way the newcomers will become accepted by the Melanesians, although it looks like being a long-drawn-out affair.

MELANESIAN CHARACTERISTICS

Solomon Islanders vary as much physically as they do in character, but one can say in general that the average Melanesian is not tall, seldom much more than 5ft 4 or 5in, that he is muscular, the result of physical toil, and that he is well built, with a great deal of dexterity. The men of the interior tend to be shorter and sturdier than the coastal dwellers and to have more stamina, whereas the coastal or salt-water people excel as swimmers and canoeists. In colour Melanesians range from coal black to light brown, the darker skins being found in the west although some Malatia people are very black, and most of them have broad noses and fuzzy hair.

Solomon Islanders on the whole are reserved and proud, but very hospitable. The majority are fair-minded and charitable, prepared to think the best of people, but even today they know little of the world outside their own village or island. When they judge a man to be wanting then he does not have a pleasant time. The worst insult that a Melanesian can pay anyone is to call him a 'rubbish man'. A rubbish man is one who is dishonest or a sponger, who fails to observe traditional behaviour or refuses to honour racial or clan obligations. Once a man is designated thus he has few rights in community life. He may even have his wife taken away from him by another man, although among ordinary Melanesians adultery is regarded as the ultimate crime and in the old days was punishable by death.

The attitude of Melanesians to white people is ambivalent, perhaps because the majority seldom see any. On the whole, very few Europeans have 'got through' to the islanders. Most touring government officers are regarded with suspicion, often being only the bearers of bad news, or collectors of taxes. The younger district officers, of whom there is a constant turnover, receive little attention as they frequently bring contradictory advice and instructions. 'Two year no more' is the pidgin phrase commonly applied to them.

Anthropologists as a rule are regarded as a source of amusement, and the more credulous among them are taken for something of a ride, islanders delighting in making up wild stories for the notebooks of the visitors. One or two visiting academics have succeeded in establishing good relations with the people of the district in which they did their field work. Raymond Firth is remembered with affection on Tikopia, and Ian Hogbin is still asked after by the older people of north-west Guadalcanal.

Expatriate traders are appreciated for the goods they sell but disliked for what islanders regard as the exorbitant prices charged. The traders in turn claim that there is precious little profit to be made out of trading in the islands. The few remaining expatriate merchants are mostly men of the old school who have spent years in the Solomons. Most of them are a source of good stories even if one or two do work a little too hard at being 'characters'.

Missionaries are respected, especially those who live among the people. One of the most complimentary things a Melanesian can say about an expatriate is 'He eats our kai', meaning that he shares the food of his hosts and generally accepts their way of life. This is certainly true of most missionaries in the islands.

Melanesians are always pleasant to a touring 'European', this being the term locally used for any white man, whether he be British, Australian, New Zealander or American. But they are not subservient and do not expect to be patronised. Some of the older men may be shy and even a little apprehensive, possibly because of memories of pre-war days when the reaction of the authorities to a slight was to launch a punitive expedition. Even as late as the 1950s the Marching Rule movement was put down by what is delicately called in the official reports 'a show of force'. The more enlightened and sensible policy of the last decade has ensured that the younger men do not share their elders' apprehension.

c

THE SOLOMON ISLANDS

As a rule Melanesians respect ability among their own kind; the establishment of the village hierarchy is usually by effort and merit, not heredity. There is little jealousy to be encountered. A young man who has worked his way from bush village to secondary education and beyond is highly regarded.

MANY LANGUAGES

There are over sixty different languages and dialects spoken among the inhabitants of the Solomons and no one language will carry a man very far, apart from pidgin which is now the *lingua franca* of the islands—although with increasing educational facilities ordinary English is being spoken more. The most commonly used native languages are Lau, Kwara'ae and Ariari on Malaita, Ghari on Guadalcanal, and Roviana in the west. A great deal more work has yet to be done on local languages but the three main types seem to be Melanesian, Polynesian and Papuan, the first being the most widespread. The Melanesian type is divided into many dialects. On Bougainville there are at least ten; there are six on Choiseul, ten on Santa Isabel, twelve on San Cristobal, and so on. Some of these dialects are related but many are not. Vocabularies seem well developed; there are over 6,000 words in the Ulawa language, for example, and this seems fairly typical.

The three Papuan languages, which are thought to be older than the Melanesian, are those of Savo and of the Russell Islands and the Vekalo tongue of Vella Lavella in the west. There are five Polynesian languages and these are spoken on the outlying islands of Tikopia, Ontong Java, Sikaiana, Anuta, and Rennell and Bellona, these last two sharing the same language.

Among the researchers who have attempted to catalogue the Melanesian languages are H. I. Hogbin, C. E. Fox and C. H. Allen, and they agree that the Melanesian dialects may be divided as follows :

Choiseul:	Bambatana, Tavula, Warisi, Rivio, Senga, Keruqala, Katupika
Shortlands:	Mono
New Georgia:	Narovo, Duke, Kusage, Baniata, Ugele, Roviana, Barake, Vangunu, Marovo
Santa Isabel:	Bugotu, Gao, Maringe, Konaga, Kakatio, Zazao, Zabana, Lagu
Floridas:	Nggela
Guadalcanal:	Ghari, Lenglo, Birao
Malaita:	To'obaita, Lau, Baelalea, Baegu'u, Fataleka, Kwara'ae, Langa Langa, Koio, Ariari, Small Mala
San Cristobal:	Arosi, Bauro, Hegaa, Funarite, Taurarafa, Oa Rafa, Mamarego, Haununu, Ugi, Ulawa
Santa Cruz:	Ndeni, Nabualue, Reefs, Taumako
Utupua:	Amba, Abago, Atago
Vanikolo:	Buma

In an investigation into the five chief languages of the main island of Malaita, W. G. Ivens came to the conclusion that they were all related with the possible exception of Ariari which rejects the sounds b, d, g, l, q, and the nasalised m and n. The language of Marau Sound on Guadalcanal (a settlement that originally came from Malaita) also resembles the dialects of Malaita. Though the intonation may be different, the people of these different language areas of Malaita can usually understand or, as they say, 'hear' each other when they meet. Ivens also pointed out that as a rule islanders who for some reason dwelt among those of another language continued to speak their own language and seemed to get by quite well.

THE VILLAGE

The typical Solomon Islander lives in a tiny village, receives a few years of primary schooling and supports himself and his family from gardens in his tribal land and by fishing from his dug-out canoe. He has not been slow to offer work for wages, to acquire iron tools, and to equip his canoe with an outboard motor. Today, a few people have chosen to adopt an urban life and have settled in Honiara. But it is in the villages that most islanders are born, live and die. With the exception of a few purchased tools, the occasional kerosene lamp, a radio set and, for the well-to-do, an outboard motor on some canoes, the majority of villagers exist as their ancestors have done for generations.

Few Solomon Island villages are large. A population of about a hundred people is average and a settlement of more than two hundred would be considered large and important. It is not unknown for the inhabitants to move a village bodily to a fresh site if the supply of arable garden land diminishes or a river floods its banks too often for safety. Keeping to the traditions of the past, villages are sited with an eye to defence against possible attack : a salt-water or coastal village may be well screened from the sea by trees, while a bush village is usually on a hill. Most villages are close to a stream or river providing an adequate supply of fresh water, but occasionally wells are bored. In addition to the permanent or semi-permanent villages there are also some temporary dwelling places, consisting usually of a few houses close to garden land which is too far away from a village to allow easy daily access, or shelters on the beach for fishermen.

Most villages are so constructed that the houses face each other in two lines with a path down the middle. A large village may have several such avenues. In every sizeable village there is usually a church, often a school and sometimes a number of custom, or ceremonial, houses. These last may include a men's house or club house, and sometimes a dwelling where the women sleep. In a number of villages, particularly on Santa Isabel, an empty house is set aside for passing strangers to sleep in.

Houses vary in size and shape but the method of construction is usually the same. Light poles lashed together with coconut fronds are used for rafters and framework, the walls are usually of bamboo or thatch and the roof is almost always thatched with the leaves of the sago palm. A ridge pole supports the rafters, and is kept in position by a number of central posts. A fairly large family house is usually rectangular in shape, about 20ft by 10ft, and divided into several rooms by wooden walls or partitions. There is perhaps a veranda, either at one end of the house or running along its length.

The floor may be of beaten earth or it may be a thatched structure or even made of betel-nut bark or wooden planks. Some houses are supported on stilts a few feet off the ground, or high up over water. The point of building a house on piles on land is to utilise uneven ground. There are few or no windows in most houses; a hole in the roof facilitates the escape of smoke if a fire is maintained, but most buildings have a separate kitchen, sometimes attached to the main dwelling house or a few yards away from it. These kitchens are utilitarian affairs, roughly thatched and containing a fire hole or a pile of stones on which the cooking is carried out.

The more ornate buildings in a village—men's houses, club houses, churches—are sometimes constructed of stouter material than the ordinary dwellings and their posts may be elaborately carved and decorated with mother-of-pearl shell. A few villages contain buildings made of sawn planks and roofed with corrugated iron; these usually belong to people who have sold a cash crop and have been able to purchase these materials, or to workers returning from the town or a plantation with wages to spend. The authorities are keen to persuade villages to buy the materials and construct their own permanent low-cost houses of fibro-cement and cement brick, and are prepared to sell the basic 'kits'. Outside Honiara few such houses have yet been built.

Among less orthodox constructions are the tree houses on Santa Isabel, although most of these were built some long time ago, probably as refuges. Bishop Patteson visiting one in the nineteenth century described it as being over 90ft above the ground, and approached from a fortified rock by a ladder. This house was 18ft long, 10ft wide and 8ft high.

The furnishings of houses are simple and functional. Sometimes there are a number of raised platforms on which mats can be placed to serve as beds. Occasionally a chair is produced for a guest, particularly for a European, but as a rule the occupants sit on the floor. They eat from the floor in many cases, although tables and similar raised surfaces are becoming more common, particularly in the houses of schoolteachers, medical assistants and other wage-earners. Most villagers possess a few purchased cooking pots and plates, and commercially manufactured articles are taking the place of the local wooden food bowls, except in the villages of the interior. Shells are used as scrapers in the preparation of vegetables and coconuts.

The fireplace, which is sometimes in the dwelling house but which may be in a separate kitchen building, is in the form of an earthen oven. This is simply a hole in the ground lined with stones upon which a few sticks are placed. Today, with stores in most districts, matches are usually used to start the fire but the traditional method of rubbing a small piece of hard wood against a large piece of soft wood is also used. After a fire has blazed for a time the hot stones are raked out until they present a level surface. The food to be cooked—usually fish, meat or vegetables—is wrapped in leaves and placed on top of the stones. More hot stones are put on top of the food. Everything is then covered with large leaves to form an effective oven. Sometimes a whole pig is cooked in a specially constructed pit in this fashion, but the average family meal can be cooked in an hour or so.

SOCIAL ORGANISATION

The most important unit in the social organisation of the Solomons is the family. The structure of this unit differs from island to island. On Santa Isabel, Bougainville and parts of Guadalcanal the system is matrilineal and inheritance is through the

38

mother's line, not the father's. The social organisation in these areas is fairly loose and wide-ranging as the young men are encouraged to seek mates outside their own groups as long as the woman's clan is one that has social affinities with the man's. In such organisations the mother's brother is an important member of the family, sometimes more important than the 'true father', as he is called.

In most areas of Malaita the patrilineal system obtains. Family groups here tend to be closer knit and the people are very clannish and suspicious of outsiders. The Polynesians also have a patrilineal system, although of a less rigid nature. In some areas, in Santa Anna in the east, for example, an admixture of Melanesian and Polynesian social systems holds sway.

The most commonly found tribal community is the clan, made up of a number of families, sharing a common language and culture. The members of a clan regard themselves as being descended from a common ancestor, although this may be a mythical figure, in the case of most clans a bird or animal, which creature must never be hunted by them. The spread of Christianity has done a great deal to minimise these beliefs in animal or bird totems, but they still exist even inside the mission sphere of influence. In some areas the shark, while not necessarily a totem figure, is believed to be the reincarnation of an ancestor, and is accorded great respect.

The main possession of the individual and of the group is land. Members of different tribes can sometimes be bound together by a common interest in a piece of land. Such an organisation is not as demanding of its members as a family or clan, but, even so, membership of it has its own obligations.

Within the family unit, especially in the matrilineal system, an islander generally regards his uncles and mother's cousins as his 'fathers' as well as the man who sired him, his 'true father', and in the same way a man refers to his cousins as his brothers or sisters. Ties within a clan are close and a 'one-talk' will always help a fellow member in any way, whether it be by helping him to build a house, offering him shelter or giving him food upon request. To refuse the request of a 'one-talk' is to bring much shame upon oneself and one's clan. Families do not always share the same house; custom in this differs from island to island. In parts of the west parents live in the same house as their younger children, while older boys and the bachelors share a common house. In the bush of Malaita even married men and women generally sleep in houses designated for each sex.

Those Melanesians who adhere to the traditional way of life, and these are still in the majority, usually marry before they are twenty, although on Malaita, where young bachelors leave for long periods in search of paid employment, the average age of marriage is later, sometimes not until the age of thirty. In non-Christian areas matches are arranged by parents while their children are still young, and even in Christian areas marriages of young people are usually negotiated by both sets of parents, the couple having little to say in the matter. In this way a young man or woman is certain to marry into a suitable clan or family and the social structure is maintained.

By custom, once a marriage has been agreed in principle the prospective groom must then pay his future in-laws for his bride. The traditional bride-price consists of shell-money—or in Santa Cruz red-feather money—pigs and porpoise teeth; and in these days it can also be paid in hard cash. On Malaita twenty to fifty strings of shell money were once paid for a bride. Today the Church, while not wishing to see the customs disappear, has in some places set a maximum of five strings of shell money for the bride-price; formerly a young man could put himself and his family deeply in debt in order to secure enough shell money and pigs to buy a wife. In pagan areas a man may still have more than one wife if he can afford it.

Solomon Islanders are quick to point out that the buying and selling of wives in this fashion is not a sign that women are held in low regard, but rather of the value placed upon them. A woman does much of the work in any family, whether as a

40

daughter or a wife. She is a most important economic unit, not only bearing and raising children but working in the gardens, cooking, cleaning and undertaking a variety of tasks. Any family losing a daughter must be compensated by the family which is going to receive her as a daughter-in-law.

Leadership plays an important part in the social structure of the Solomon Islands. Among Melanesians (who are unlike the Polynesians in this respect) there is little hereditary leadership. Instead, the 'big man' cult holds sway. Within any village community the 'big man' is the one who shows greatest evidence of wealth by giving lavish feasts and making spectacular sacrifices to the spirits. Often more than one man in a community will seek this position and there will be intense competition to see which of them can grow the most food or sell the most copra in order to give the biggest feast and impress most people. The title of 'big man' can change hands quite often if enough people are interested enough to seek the honour. By becoming the local leader a man automatically becomes a sort of unpaid magistrate, settling disputes and making decisions.

The 'big man' cult has occasionally been disturbed by the government's practice of appointing official paid headmen in the districts. Sometimes the appointed headman is the 'big man', so all is well. At other times, however, a headman is appointed by the authorities because of his knowledge of English or pidgin, or because he has worked for a time in Honiara and can converse without embarrassment with expatriate government officers. In such cases, Solomon Islanders aver, although the official headman may act as a go-between, it is the big man who makes the decisions, after discussion with other villagers, and it is the big man who retains the real power in a district.

It is difficult to become a big man without possessing wealth, and in the Solomons wealth is judged by material possessions and especially by the amount of land owned, particularly if it is well worked, productive and profitable. Land tenure is a complicated matter, and the cause of many disputes. As a rule land is held on

41

a family or clan basis, although house and garden areas may be handed down from mother or father according to local usage. Within a clan area, a man who clears land and plants it can be considered the owner of it, at least for his lifetime and that of his sons. But tradition and custom so complicate matters that on one small piece of land it is quite possible, to quote an extreme example, for one man to own the land, another to own the trees, and a third to own the fruit on the trees. It is not always easy to discover who exactly does own any particular plot, and this was the cause of a great deal of bitterness in the early days between islanders and expatriate traders and planters who purchased local land. The expatriates bought the land freehold, while the islanders assumed that local tradition would be followed and that upon the death of the man who had sold the land it would revert to the clan.

The sea cannot be owned by anyone in the Solomons, but the off-shore fishing rights on a particular stretch of coast may be jealously guarded by the inhabitants, and a reef may be the personal property of a man or family.

VILLAGE ECONOMY

Solomon Islanders, with the exception of the town-dwellers, depend for their food on agriculture, fishing and hunting. If any actual cash is available rice and tinned meat may be bought from local stores. Bottled beer, too, is a very popular purchase.

The men clear the ground and prepare the gardens and the women plant the root crops, generally yams, taro and sweet potatoes. Both men and women maintain the gardens, weeding and generally looking after the plot, but the women do most of the gathering of the vegetables. Each family has its own garden on the land owned by the clan. The larger the family, the bigger the garden and the more food produced—and consumed, of course. Bananas and coconuts are harvested, but apart from planting the trees in the first place no great cultivation or maintenance is needed. Bush oranges, limes, pineapples, man-goes and paw-paws are also grown. In some areas a little tobacco is grown and one or two islanders on Guadalcanal have been known to grow coffee, but mainly as a cash crop. Various nuts, including the ubiquitous betel-nut, are grown. With the exception of Polynesian Sikaiana and Ontong Java, which have their own forms of fermented coconut juice, there is no indigenous alcoholic drink in the Solomons, water being the main liquid consumed.

The Solomon seas are rich in fish and the coastal people catch and eat large numbers as part of their basic diet. Various methods of fishing are used : hooks and lines, with and without bait, are popular; great skill is shown with bow and arrow; spear-fishing by the light of torches at night is common. In many districts nets attached to a frame are scooped into the sea, and in the eastern islands there is a curious form of fishing by which a kite flown from a canoe in turn drops a line and hook into the sea. Basket fishing is another method adopted, as is the strictly illegal prac-tice of throwing dynamite and similar explosives into rivers to stun the fish. The most prized fish is the bonito, with the tuna in second place. Shark is not highly regarded nor are flying fish, but turtles, porpoises and dugong are considered delicacies.

Pigs are kept—the number a man owns is a sign of his wealth. Both coastal dwellers and bush people also hunt wild pigs with dogs and spears. Chickens are kept in most villages; birds and flying foxes are trapped with nets or shot with arrows and eaten. Barter is decreasing in the islands, although pigs and stick tobacco are still used as items of exchange. Today Australian currency, which is the official one in the protectorate, has found its way even to the remoter islands, but some of the older men still possess the gold sovereigns which were once in use, and there are stories of Santa Cruz people owning stores of gold coins, once the property of the first Spanish explorers, but these rumours have never been confirmed. A few French coins have been discovered in the eastern Solomons and it is possible that they were brought to the area in the eighteenth century by La Pérouse and his men on that ill-fated expedition when the French navigator lost his ships off Vanikolo.

Traditional shell money is still used in many areas, as are porpoise teeth and, in some areas, the teeth of the flying fox. The shell money consists of small discs made of red or white shell, each disc less than half an inch in diameter, and strung on lengths of bush twine, each about a fathom long and, in fact, always referred to as a fathom. Fathoms may be broken off into shorter lengths to buy smaller items. Shell money is still manufactured, especially on Malaita, but much of it is inherited, being handed down from father to son—though the older traditional strings are now rare. In 1971, £20 was being offered on Malaita for a fathom of shell money by traders who were having little difficulty in re-selling it at £50 a string.

The red-feather money of Santa Cruz was made from the red feathers of the honey bird and the brown feathers of a dove. Coils of this currency are about 30yd long and 2in wide, and the feathers of about 500 birds are needed for one coil. Red-feather money is still manufactured on demand but the prospective purchaser has first to agree terms with the three old men who are the hereditary manufacturers. One catches the honey bird; the second constructs individual platelets of dove or pigeon feathers and then adds the red down; and the third joins the platelets together by binding them on two cords to make the coil.

With the development of a cash economy and a gradual improvement in communications, islanders have been increasingly engaged in buying and selling goods, thus encouraging the development of local manufacturing industries on a small scale. The largest of these industries is the manufacture of copra. This is the basic cash product of the country and over half the total production comes from individual smallholdings. Islanders are well versed in the arts of clearing land and planting and the soil of the coastal areas is suited to the growth of coconut palms. The largest holding is that of Lever Brothers who own a number of plantations, most of them controlled by expatriate staff. There are still a number of expatriates who own single plantations on different islands but most of these are producing less and less copra as the trees grow old and are not replaced. The production of copra from native holdings, on the other hand, is steadily increasing. This can vary from the efforts of a single man cutting the flesh of his coconuts in half and drying it in a primitive smoke-house to the combined work of a large family which has purchased a commercial copra dryer and can thus produce a higher grade of the finished product.

Some men make canoes for sale, and wood-carvings, baskets and woven work are the usual village industries but these are only found in some villages. The wood carving can be of a very high standard, although work of an inferior quality is beginning to reach Honiara. Some of the older craftsmen produce beautiful models of birds, animals and human figures, and intricately carved walking sticks. Representations of creatures that are half-animal and half-human are popular, especially the *kareimanu*, half-shark, half-man. War clubs, slightly less than life-size, are a speciality of the carvers of Rennell and Bellona. When the first explorers to reach the Solomons saw clubs of this sort they thought they were decorated with gold, but this was probably shell inlay work which is often used today as an embellishment on carvings.

Tourists visiting Honiara usually buy a carving of some sort as a souvenir, but artefacts of cultural significance like shell money and the older traditional carvings are not allowed to leave the country.

GETTING ABOUT

Outside the capital and the district stations a Solomon Islander usually has to walk if he wishes to get anywhere; to the interior at any rate the main means of progress is by bush track from village to village. Islanders can walk long distances without fatigue if they have to, but they usually have to have a good reason for doing so. Coastal dwellers dislike going into the interior

45

and the cold (by their standards) mountain regions, and certainly for long, sustained activity in this difficult terrain the bushmen are far superior to the salt-water men. Mountain dwellers can carry loads of up to 40lb in comparative comfort for long distances. The women are even better at it than the men; it is in fact the custom for the women to carry burdens, leaving the men with their hands free in case of attack.

When travelling by sea the salt-water people come into their own. Practically every man has his own canoe or ready access to one. In former times canoes were constructed with tools of shell, but now that iron and steel tools are available they take less time to build. Most islanders can turn their hands to making their own, but some specialise in it and sell their products. Prices vary from district to district. A small one-man canoe can cost anything between four and twelve Australian dollars, while larger canoes can fetch up to sixty dollars and more. The commonest type is single hulled and light, constructed of planks lashed to ribs by means of cleats. The nut of *Parinarium laurinum* is used for sealing the seams, and the outside is painted, partly for decoration and partly as an additional precaution against leaks. Sometimes, and particularly on the larger canoes, the bows are decorated with mother-of-pearl designs and carvings. The single-outrigger canoe is also built, especially in the eastern district. The outrigger is joined to the hull by two booms which are lashed to it with vines or rope. Occasionally, on the opposite side to the outrigger a balancing platform juts out over the water. The simplest canoes are the dug-outs used on rivers and on the calm waters of lagoons, and the smallest are the 3ft models built by fathers for their children.

Many canoes are equipped with a makeshift sail; sometimes this consists merely of a pole stuck through a crossbar, with one end of the sail attached to the pole and the other held by an occupant of the craft, but to take advantage of a sudden favourable wind all sorts of things can be used, from shirts to large leaves.

46

The magnificent war canoes once used on head-hunting expeditions were about 60ft in length with a beam of 5ft and a depth amidships of 3ft, the bows and stern much decorated with carvings and shell work, curving to as much as 13ft. San Cristobal in the east and the New Georgia Islands in the west made some of the most splendid. They were capable of carrying thirty to forty men, one of them usually beating time as the others paddled. Few sights are more impressive or awe-inspiring than a war canoe of this sort approaching a beach. The war canoes were kept in special canoe houses and jealously guarded, but unhappily not many of them survived the early years of European rule. Those that did are now used on ceremonial occasions.

Solomon Islanders seem completely unafraid of the sea. The war canoes were capable of going on long-range raiding missions, and the men of Santa Cruz and the outer eastern islands travelled—and still do travel—long distances, out of sight of land for days at a time and steering at night by the stars. Some long journeys are inadvertent: a sudden squall or storm can drive a canoe off course for hundred of miles, but the occupants usually sight land eventually, though they may have to wait for a government vessel to pick them up and return them to their home island.

But the islanders are not reluctant to use more modern forms of transport where these are available. Roads are being built, though slowly; government vessels ply the coasts on scheduled and non-scheduled trips; and there is a small internal airline connecting the capital with district stations. These developments are discussed in chapter 7.

RELIGION

Christian missions of various denominations have been active in the Solomons for a hundred years, and most of the protectorate is today Christian, although there are still pagan areas, especially on Malaita. Originally the missions had separate spheres of influence, but today different denominations work close to each other on the same islands. Religious life is an important part of any Christian community in the Solomons. Practically every village has its church and its catechist or priest; every day begins and ends with a service.

The main denominations working in the Solomons are the Roman Catholics, Anglicans (Melanesian Mission), South Sea Evangelicals, the United Church (formerly Methodist), and the Seventh Day Adventists. The Baha'i Church has also entered the Solomons in recent years. Most denominations support the Solomon Islands Christian Association, and a remarkable feature of religious life in the Solomons is the amount of co-operation existing between different denominations at all levels.

The average Solomon Islander is extremely devout and does his best to live his life according to Christian principles; his faith is a very real thing to him. In many areas, however, the Christian faith is carried on, in all sincerity, in tandem with some of the old pagan beliefs which have been retained. The cult of ancestors was an integral part of the old religion, and this remains. The spirits of the dead may be contacted and called upon to help in adversity. Sometimes the spirit of a dead man lives for a time in the body of a shark or an animal, and such a creature is *tabu*. There are also other spirits, which were never alive but exist all round the living. In order to approach any spirit the services of a priest of the pagan variety or of a member of the village who has inherited the right to talk to the spirits, must be obtained.

The concept of *mana* is strong. Mana is spiritual power and a man or woman who has it can do almost anything. On the other hand, mana can also mean fate; if something good or bad happens to someone it is because of his mana. Ancestral spirits are always watching and waiting. Any breach of custom is noticed and deplored. Ancestral spirits do not always have any particular home, but the less effective spirits usually occupy some tangible place, a pool or stream perhaps.

Many islanders still believe firmly in magic and magicians.

Page 49 Honiara, capital of the group: *(above)* from the air with wharf; *(below)* the main thoroughfare at the rush hour

Page 50 Government: *(above)* district station of Eastern District at Kirakira, with typical government touring vessel at anchor and the airstrip across the bay; *(below)* Gizo, administrative centre of the Western District

Some areas still contain *vele* men, magicians who inherit their powers from a father or an uncle. A vele man can put a curse on an enemy or a malefactor and unless the latter has a stronger magic or can find someone who possesses superior powers of this order, disaster and even death may strike.

Cannibalism was originally bound up with pagan religion, particularly with the idea of mana. By eating one's enemy his (or her) mana could sometimes be obtained. In other areas cannibalism served merely as an expression of contempt for the dead man. The idea that Solomons cannibalism originated because of a protein deficiency in the local diet has been largely discredited. In the head-hunting days, human life was extremely cheap. Human sacrifices were common, the most gruesome taking place upon the occasion of the launching of a new war canoe : enemies taken prisoner in battle were tied up and laid in ranks on a slope to form a human slipway. The canoe, with its sharp hull, was then launched over the prisoners down to the sea, tearing them to pieces in the process. Sacrifices were also made as an act of propitiation if the spirits were thought to be angry; sometimes a pig would be offered, or in extreme cases a man or woman would be thrown to the sharks or otherwise disposed of.

Clubs and societies were once an important part of the religious life of the Solomons. Club houses still exist today and are often tabu to women and girls, but usually serve no other purpose than a storehouse for objects of religious significance. Initiation rites at puberty still take place for both boys and girls in some districts, but these seem less common than in the past, perhaps because so many boys and girls now leave home and go to boarding schools for their senior primary education.

Pagans as well as Christians believe in an afterlife in the Solomons. Most burials follow the normal pattern and there are burial grounds in or close to most villages. Sometimes the practice of cremation is followed, and some salt-water people dispose of the dead in the sea after an appropriate ceremony. Sometimes the skulls of important people are kept in the village custom house; in the old days the skulls of enemies were similarly displayed, often attached to poles.

WARFARE AND WEAPONS

Melanesians are proud people and think highly of a good fighter. There are no written records of their early history but there is a strong oral tradition of fights and fighting. Blood feuds were carried on for generations and there have always been traditional inter-island and inter-clan rivalries. In most areas the bushmen and the salt-water people were always skirmishing. Putting down this endemic warfare was one of the major tasks of the British administration, and it was not until shortly before World War II that Malaita was brought under control in this respect. Today brawls between bush people and coastal dwellers occasionally take place, but the weapons used seem to be fists and stones and nothing worse results than a few headaches and a fine by a native court.

The head-hunting raids of the Roviana people and those of the eastern district were greatly feared, especially as these were sometimes disguised as missions of friendship. A raiding party would land on an island, pretend to put on a dance or an entertainment for a village, and then fall on the spectators and kill them. Professional murderers abounded. C. E. Fox mentions them as being in existence on San Cristobal at the beginning of this century, and the *ramos* or professional murderers of Malaita were particularly feared.

Weapons, as well as being effective, were also often very beautifully designed. Bows were usually made of palm wood, with vegetable fibre for the strings. Arrows, generally not feathered, were of cane with points of hard wood or human bone. Islanders today insist that these arrows were often poisoned, but B. A. L. Cranstone in *Melanesia: A Short Ethnography*, says that this is not so and that substances smeared on the heads, which did in fact often cause tetanus, were put there for magical reasons. Throwing-spears, today used mainly for hunting fish, were once a formidable part of the armoury of a Solomon Islands warrior. These throwing-spears often had bamboo shafts and hardwood heads, while thrusting spears were usually one-piece weapons, constructed of hardwood. Shields were often carried; those on Santa Isabel were constructed of wicker or wood, with much ornate shell work. Carved from a single piece of wood, war clubs also were often marvels of craftsmanship, some so beautiful that they must have been used mainly for display and ceremonial occasions.

Stone axes, the head thrust into a wooden handle or lashed to it with fibre, were used for both fighting and domestic purposes, and knives of stone were also used before traders began to bring the steel variety with them to barter for local goods. For a time unscrupulous traders used also to offer rifles, especially the Snider, as an item of exchange. Today a firearms licence has to be obtained before a rifle can be owned.

MUSIC AND THE ARTS

Storytelling is still an important part of village life, tales of ancestors and the 'time before' predominating. Music, too, is popular, although the introduction of transistor radios has resulted in traditional music becoming less widespread. Country and western-type music is very much in favour with the younger men and women, who regard the old custom songs as being old-fashioned and rather silly. Hundreds of record requests are received by the broadcasting service every week. Easily the most popular expatriate singer is an Australian country and western artiste, Slim Dusty. Songs in pidgin by local singer-composers like Jim Baku and Fred Maedola are great favourites on the radio. They deal with contemporary events and personalities. One of Baku's most popular numbers is 'Technical Week Long Auki', which tells of the arrival of schoolchildren at the district station to be shown over the various government departments there. Maedola's most requested song is probably 'Lucky Girl', which tells in pidgin of a young lady who goes from boy to boy; another popular one is 'Time Me Sick Long Number Nine', number nine being the pidgin description of the Honiara hospital. These songs are simple with a heavy country and western beat and represent a fusion of expatriate culture and local life and conditions.

Some custom songs are still quite well known in their districts; most are in local dialects and deal with well-known events— the war, floods and storms, and so on. Some songs are of the 'saga' variety, telling of folk heroes, but now and again real people feature in them, one of these being Nori who was one of the leaders of Marching Rule (see chapter 6). One well-known custom song of recent years is in pidgin and deals with the Japanese invasion. It is called 'Japani Ha-ha', and some of the verses go like this :

> Mi fulae olobauti, longo isti long westi
> Mi sendere olo rouni keepim Solomoni.
> Me worka luka luka longo landi long sea
> Ha ha ! ha ha ! Japani ha ha !

> Iamu eaforse, mi saena longo hemu
> Because biki fiti comu longo Japani
> Me lookimu woni fala samaringi daeva downi
> Ha ha ! Ha ha ! Japani ha ha !

> Mifela comu downi longo mi parasuti
> Enemi sooti comu but misi olobauti
> You reeremu comu but where mi longu bemu
> Ha ha ! Ha ha ! Japani ha ha !

The song is supposed to be the war chant of a Solomon Islander fighting for the Allies against the Japanese and expressing his contempt for the enemy as well as boasting about his own fighting prowess. The tune is a catchy one, a rough translation of the words above would be :

I fly everywhere, to east and to west.
I keep watch all around, guarding the Solomons.
My duty is to look over the land and the sea.
Ha ha ! Ha ha ! Japanese, ha ha !

I join the airforce, I sign to work for them.
Because the big war came with the Japanese.
I look for the submarines which dive under the sea.
Ha ha ! Ha ha ! Japanese, ha ha !

I come down with my parachute.
The enemy shoots but misses me.
He looks for me everywhere but can't find me.
Ha ha ! Ha ha ! Japanese, ha ha !

In the more traditional style music is made through pan pipes, which are bundles of bamboo or reed pipes lashed together; by castanets or rattles, usually consisting of nuts or seeds gathered on a string and worn round the ankle and beaten by constant stamping; and by drums beaten by hand. Conch shells are usually used for calling people together or as a form of signalling rather than for providing music.

Other art forms include wood carving, which we have already touched upon; weaving and mat making; the latter is particularly well done in the east, and Tikopian mats are sought after by inhabitants of most other islands. There exists no native tradition of written literature or painting.

ARTIFICIAL ISLANDS

One of the most unusual sights of the Solomons are the artificial or man-made islands in the Lau and Langa Langa lagoons of Malaita and at Taumako in the eastern islands. They have been constructed on shoal passages from coral boulders transported from the reef. Most of them are overcrowded and built to no apparent pattern, and the majority are surrounded by individual houses on stilts. Artificial islands are still being constructed today.

As a rule a family or a young married couple will build an island big enough for one or two houses and then add to it as it becomes necessary. First stones are assembled and piled upon the reef and then ferried by raft to the chosen site, which is usually marked at each corner by a tall pole. After many laborious journeys from the reef the mound of rocks is built up to a height between 6 and 10ft above the surface. The builders then transport sand from the mainland to fill in the holes between the rocks.

When all this has been done it is time to build the houses and perhaps also a pen to hold some pigs. There will be no water supply, except for rain, and although one or two palm trees may eventually grow, all food has to be transported from gardens on the mainland. Building an island is a slow process. Dr C. E. Fox, who lived on Malaita for some years, tells of seeing a man and his wife construct a small island in six months, but the majority of island dwellers when questioned about their homes insist that an artificial island takes at least a year to build, even with the asistance of friends and relatives.

There is a division of opinion about the original reason for building such islands. Old people in the Lau and Langa Langa lagoons say that they were built to provide safety from the attacks of the bush dwellers, but anthropologists largely discount this. A more popular theory is that the islands were built as a refuge from the mosquitoes on the shore. W. G. Ivens, who made a study of the Lau area, suggested that Sulufou was originally built as a convenient dwelling place close to the market, and that other artificial islands were later constructed by people who admired the original island and wanted to copy it.

Sulufou is certainly the largest and oldest of the artificial islands of the Lau Lagoon. It is about 80yd long and 30yd wide, situated, like all the others, between the reef and the shore. The lagoon is about 30 miles long and 2 miles wide and contains some fifty of these artificial islands.

The rocks most favoured for the building of the islands are the large smooth ones found on the floor of the lagoon, but as most of these have been used up over the years the more jagged rocks from the reef itself have to be used today. The rocks on the shore are not favoured, as they are inclined to crumble. Sometimes an artificial island is built around a large rock already present in the lagoon. Sulufou was the first entirely artificial island to be built up on the lagoon floor, and the man who is thought to have been responsible for it, Leo, is still talked about with admiration.

The smaller artificial islands are usually occupied by members of one family, but the larger ones may be divided among a number of families. On Sulufou, for example, there are four main families, each with its traditional anchorage. Unlike most other parts of Malaita the Lau area maintains the hereditary principle of leadership. A man becomes a chief because he is the descendant of chiefs. Such a position is now largely formal. Once the chiefs were the wealthy men of the lagoon area who owned all the fishing rights and also the fishing nets, but this is no longer the case. A great deal of respect is still paid to them, but they do little more than decree when feasts may be held, and settle occasional matters of dispute, usually over garden land on the mainland where island dwellers have earned the right to make gardens either by clearing forest land or by marrying women from the coastal strip who own land there. Today there is no paramount chief of the lagoon, although less than fifty years ago the smaller chiefs would gather together to select a big chief or *aofia* from the ranks of the existing chiefs or their sons. The main task of the aofia was to maintain peace among the people of the lagoon. It was essential that the man selected for the post should be of gentle disposition; by custom after his election he was never allowed to enter the place where traditional sacrifices for war were offered. Sometimes the aofia would also be a priest concerned with ancestor worship; it was certainly believed that if fighting broke out among the people of the artificial islands the ghosts of the ancestors of the lagoon people would kill the aofia.

Some of the older men still remember the ceremony of appointing the aofia. After all the chiefs had agreed on who was to become the paramount chief a special feast was held. During this feast a priest would hang the skin of an areca nut, the symbol of peace, from the ear of the new aofia in the presence of representatives from every artificial island. The aofia was also presented with a gourd in which a stick was inserted. By rattling the stick in the gourd the aofia reminded people of his presence and his function.

Marriage in the Lau Lagoon area still follows the pattern described by Ivens in 1930. The father of a boy of marriageable age looks for a suitable girl for his son. This process is known as *iroa geni*. When the girl has been selected the father makes a down payment of one piece of shell money to her parents. Both fathers then negotiate the final bride price. The going rate for a girl is usually known by both parties and each father has a pretty good idea in advance what the final agreed figure will be. When a sum of shell money has been decided upon the discussion is ended.

As soon as the prospective groom's family has gathered the bride-price together word is sent to the girl's family that a party will come to collect her on a certain date. The groom-to-be is not included in the party, but the bride-price is taken in the canoes and the mother of the groom also takes a certain amount of cloth with her as a present for the mother of the bride. No member of the visiting party wears ornaments : by custom, these would be seized and retained by girls in the bride's family. On landing there is always a mock battle on the shore. Sticks, stones and wooden spears are used in this conflict and sometimes the younger men on each side get carried away in their enthusiasm and cuts and bruises result before the chief of the island decides that it is time to break the scuffle up. The next stage in the proceedings is for a male member of the groom's party to display the bride-price, ostentatiously counting the number of strings. A man from the bride's family takes the money from him and hangs the bride-price up on display. Then the groom's mother hands a fathom of shell money and some cloth to the bride's mother.

The bride is adorned in her finery, consisting of decorated combs in her hair, a necklace of porpoise teeth and bracelets of trochus shell around her arms, and these she continues to wear until the time of her wedding. Then, accompanied by her father and some of the younger members of her own family, she departs for the bridegroom's island. As the bride steps ashore her future mother-in-law walks in front of her, putting pandanus mats on the ground so that the girl's feet never touch the earth. This entitles the girl to claim later that she walked on new mats and that she was not stolen from her home. A custom feast follows, the food being provided by the girl's father. Young people from neighbouring islands are invited to the feast which goes on all night. Then the girl, with some of her brothers and sisters, spends the next six months with her prospective in-laws, helping with household tasks but not sleeping with her husband-to-be. In this way the two get to know each other and lose their shyness. Then the girl goes back to her home island and waits to be summoned to the actual wedding ceremony, when a huge feast is held on the island of the bride's family, presents are exchanged and finally the bride and groom go to live in the house of the groom's parents, the latter moving into another house.

There are government-run and mission clinics on the mainland of Malaita, but many women of the artificial islands still follow the traditional customs pertaining to the birth of children. Once the island of Adagege was used as a maternity island for the women of Sulufou but today the women from many of the artificial islands go to the mainland to deliver their children. During the actual birth the mother must not be touched by any of the women attending her; she cuts the umbilical cord herself after the birth but does not tie it up. She then wraps the baby in pandanus leaves and goes back to her village, propelling herself and her baby on a small raft, escorted by canoes paddled by the other women. The mother and baby spend thirty days in the

59

bisi, or women's house, during which time the woman has to observe traditional dietary requirements, eating only special taro and no large fish. On the thirtieth day she may leave the bisi with her child. A special feast is held in her honour but no married men may attend it.

When the child has been weaned and is old enough to be looked after by the older women of the island the mother takes up her normal duties again. These include the day-to-day work in the gardens which have been established by the men. It is the job of the women to cut up the trees which have been felled by the men during the preparation of the site and then to burn the wood. They then visit the gardens regularly, grubbing up the taros which are ready to be eaten and the next day replanting the tops of the taro they have consumed.

The women also collect water for the island from the mainland. This they do in hollow bamboo rods some 2ft in length and blocked at one end, carrying as many as twenty of these at a time on their backs. Firewood too must be gathered and taken back to the islands by the women, all of whom can handle a canoe with skill. They cook the food over wooden fires but are not allowed to touch the fishing nets, which are spread over the rocks of the artificial island when not in use, lest they should lose virtue and catch no more fish.

A few of the artificial islands in the Lau Lagoon are still pagan but the majority are nominally Christian. This means, as in most areas in the Solomons, that Christianity is practised in tandem with the old beliefs and superstitions. Sulufou has a large and well-built church constructed of stone and timber, and most of the other islands contain a small locally built church. In addition to a Christian minister or catechist there is often a traditional priest on the island as well. On the pagan islands shark-worship is practised, some of the priests being credited with the power of summoning sharks to them.

When a man or woman of an island dies the body is buried on the island. Once corpses were buried in a sitting position with the head and shoulders left above the ground, but this practice is no longer followed. In the old days a chief was buried in his canoe in a special *beu* or men's house. Today a Christian burial is much more common and engraved headstones may be found on graves on Sulufou and some of the larger artificial islands.

POLYNESIANS IN PARTICULAR

The Polynesian islands of the Solomons are remote and have kept many of their old customs and ways of life, which differ in a number of respects from those of the Melanesian islands of the protectorate.

To the north, Ontong Java or Lord Howe Island, consists of a number of small coral islands clustered around the lagoon. Extremely isolated, and visited by government shipping only three or four times a year, Ontong Java depends upon the visits of small trading vessels arriving to collect copra to keep them even remotely in touch with the rest of the Solomons. A small radio transmitter performs intermittently, but at the time of the last cyclone it was out of action and the inhabitants were unable to appeal for help until the next copra boat arrived.

The people depend upon the sale of copra to buy trade goods from a small store on one of the islands and also upon the collection of the sea slug, bêche de mer, for the Japanese market. Transfixing the creatures underwater with a heavily weighted spear is a laborious business; it takes two or three months to collect the five tons which make up the average shipment. A few of the Ontong Java men also collect trochus shells washed up on the reef. There is a small but steady market for these in Honiara from where they are sent overseas to be polished and manufactured into simulated pearl buttons and similar decorations. The women of Ontong Java look after the gardens while the men fish.

Because the coconut palms are too precious to be felled and there are few trees of any other sort, dug-out canoes are generally made from driftwood washed ashore after storms. The holy man of the village makes the first incision of the chisel, to drive away the evil spirits; the log is then hollowed out and shaped and a type of seaweed rubbed over the hull to caulk any cracks. An outrigger float is kept in place by attached booms.

The houses of Ontong Java are less ornate than many Melanesian dwellings. A framework of poles forms the skeleton of the house, the walls consist of hangings of plaited coconut leaf attached to upright poles, and the roof is a thatch of pandanus leaves. The kitchen is often part of the main building, with a hole in the roof to let out the smoke.

The men of Ontong Java wear shorts or lap-laps while the women usually wear skirts. Many islanders of both sexes are tattooed. In childhood the upper part of the face is decorated with fish and geometrical designs, and these are extended to other parts of the body later in life. But the custom appears to be dying out, though there are still one or two practitioners of the art. Dye is made from the ash of burnt nuts, and the tattooing needle, really a number of needles fashioned from the bone of a bird and attached to a stick, is hammered into the skin with a small stick. The person being tattooed usually has to be held down during the operation.

A number of epidemics during the early decades of the twentieth century more than decimated the population of Ontong Java but, in common with the other islands of the Solomons, its population is now steadily on the increase.

Rennell and Bellona are barren and hilly islands about a hundred miles south of Guadalcanal. Like Ontong Java they are rarely visited by government ships, but recently an airstrip has been cleared on Rennell and a great deal of prospecting for bauxite has been carried out there by a Japanese firm. This island, $49\frac{1}{2}$ miles long and $8\frac{1}{2}$ miles wide is, for most of its surface, pure coral with no soil. It is difficult to grow food, but coconuts, pawpaws and sweet potatoes are produced, together with yams and a few pineapples. A few springs provide drinking water and the islanders do their best to store rainwater; there is also a large freshwater lake. Birds, especially pigeons, are hunted for food, from platforms built among the branches of trees. The hunter climbs up to a platform, covers himself with leaves and then allows a decoy pigeon on the end of a string to flutter among the branches, while he imitates the call. When a wild pigeon approaches the platform it is captured in a net.

Rennell has a long tradition of internecine war; for years the eastern and western sides of the island were in conflict with each other, and until fairly recently a man could take possession of another man's land by killing him and defending the land against his relatives. The chiefs of the island—normally there were three, known as *anggikis*—were primarily religious leaders and had no jurisdiction over land disputes. Today there are a few government-appointed headmen, and the island is entering upon a period of prosperity, selling food to the Japanese employees of the mining firm. It is expected that the islanders will get an appreciable share of the revenue from the bauxite, but that the effect of this on their way of life will be considerable.

Bellona, 6 miles by 2, with a population of about six hundred, is surrounded by sheer cliffs which drop quite abruptly inland making a depression in the centre of the island. The soil is good and the islanders grow coconuts, bananas, yams, potatoes and manioc. Some fresh water is supplied by springs in the cliffs, but this is an intermittent source and the islanders depend mainly on rainwater, cooking their food, in fact, in sea water. Like the people of Rennell, they are excitable and volatile in temperament, of good physique, and without any sense of belonging to the Solomons. Already some of the younger Rennell men are maintaining that revenue from the bauxite on their island should not have to be shared with the rest of the protectorate.

Sikaiana, another Polynesian island, lies about 130 miles east of Malaita. The island is small and crowded and its inhabitants are among the most extrovert, boisterous and handsome of all Solomon Islanders. The women are extremely beautiful and fond of dancing, while the men are renowned for their practical jokes.

The distinguished visitor to the island is lifted reverently from his canoe, carried gently through the shallows and then dropped abruptly into the sea, to the accompaniment of joyful cries from the onlookers.

Tikopia, the last of the major Polynesian islands in the group, is situated 150 miles east of Santa Cruz, and is perhaps the most isolated of all the outliers. Like Sikaiana it is an extinct volcano and its volcanic soil is very fertile. Tikopia has a large and beautiful crater lake, its sloping sides covered with tropical growth, and here the islanders fish and catch wild duck from their outrigger canoes. Professor Raymond Firth lived on the island for some years and made a study of the Tikopian culture, and was impressed by their high standard of courtesy and consideration for others.

Overcrowding has forced many of the younger Tikopians to leave their island and make fresh homes for themselves in other parts of the protectorate. This uprooting has caused some unhappiness but is acknowledged as being inevitable. This may be a hopeful portent for the future. Only as a united nation will these dignified, tolerant and delightful Solmon Islanders be able to cope with the inevitable stresses and strains of the years to come.

For the reader who is interested in detailed investigations into the separate cultures of the Solomon clans, the following regional studies (publication details on p 208) are recommended:

BLACKWOOD, B. *Both Sides of the Buka Passage* (Western Solomons)
CODRINGTON, R. H. *The Melanesians*
FIRTH, R. *We, the Tikopia*
FOX, C. E. *The Threshold of the Pacific* (San Cristobal)
IVENS, W. G. *Melanesians of the South-Eastern Solomons*
WHEELER, C. G. *Mono-Alu Folklore* (Western Solomons)

3   TIME BEFORE

THERE are no written records of life in the Solomons before the arrival of the first Europeans in the sixteenth century. In order to gain an impression of what life must have been like we must rely on the researches of a few anthropologists, the oral traditions of the islanders and the written accounts of the first Spaniards to arrive there.

Some anthropologists suggest that as a number of the languages in the Solomons have affinities with Malay, the original inhabitants of the islands may have made the sea journey to the Solomons from the west in the gradual migration of the negritos who populated New Guinea and parts of the Pacific thousands of years ago.

The next wave of visitors after the negritos probably consisted of Melanesians coming from the Malayo-Asian area in their canoes. Anthropologists tend to favour a prehistoric date for their arrival. Excavations in the Solomons have unearthed shell tools believed to date around 930 BC and this is the earliest date we have indicating life in the islands. This would appear to tie up with the statement of Brookfield and Hart in *Melanesia* that there was 'a major increase in voyaging and cultural diffusion along the north coast of New Guinea and deep into Island Melanesia between about 1000 BC and the first millennium AD'.

Today the strong division between the coastal dwellers, the salt-water people, and the men and women of the interior, the bush people, has given rise to the theory that perhaps the original

65

arrivals, the negritos, settled in the interior or were driven there by the arrival of the second wave of invaders who took up residence along the coastal fringe.

The Polynesians, it is believed, came later, settling on the outer islands after long canoe voyages from the east, driven off course by strong winds or deliberately setting forth into the unknown in search of new homes.

The islanders themselves have no legends about their arrival in the Solomons, except in the case of the Polynesians, some of whom recount tales of great voyages over unknown seas. The folk tales of the Melanesians are of comparatively recent times, and describe migrations and exploits within the islands of clan heroes, sometimes female, who are now worshipped among the assembly of ghosts and spirits. The islanders call this period 'time before'.

Even today Solomon Islanders are great tellers of stories. As Father Goerts writes: 'When darkness falls on villages, outdoor life comes to an end and indoor life begins. Talk becomes the main occupation. This is the time when the parents are alone with their children; when they have the time and the privacy to teach their children past history, moral values, and to entertain them.'

As Solomon Islanders were not literate in their own tongue until the arrival of missionaries in the nineteenth and twentieth centuries, their history has perforce been handed down in this oral tradition. There are attempts to explain the origins of the people (they are often said to be descended from sharks), stories about the occupation and settlement of land, the wars between tribes and villages over land disputes, and the development of house and canoe building, hunting, fishing, farming and gardening. We can see that almost from the beginning the people settled into an agricultural economy, living in small villages and keeping very much to themselves, developing their own customs and traditions, and treating strangers as enemies. They cultivated their gardens, growing yams, taro, coconuts and sugar cane. They

Page 67 Trade: *(above)* copra being rowed out at Santa Cruz to waiting vessel for transit to Honiara; *(below)* Viru Harbour, New Georgia, scene of a flourishing timber industry

Page 68 (above) Business and pleasure: canoes at Buala, Santa Isabel—wharf in background; (below) canoes set out from the north coast of Bellona with the trade winds blowing

fished from their canoes, carved baskets, food bowls and figures, and hunted wild pigs, crabs, turtles, birds and opossums. Celebrations and feasts were frequent and no one had to work too hard under the sun in order to live comfortably.

Some areas—Simbo in the west, for example—were particularly productive, because of the fertility of the soil. Other areas were noted for their fighting men : the approach of war canoes from the Roviana Lagoon in the west seemed to be feared by almost everyone. From the early days Malaita was known to be particularly inhospitable and none cared to be shipwrecked on the shores of this island. Head-hunting was practised on Malaita and Guadalcanal and on parts of Santa Isabel. There was also a certain amount of cannibalism but it seems fairly certain that the islanders ate the flesh of their vanquished enemies not for enjoyment but to assert their superiority over them or to gain spiritual power. Sacrifices, mainly of pigs, were offered to the spirits, usually with a great deal of ceremony. Each village had its headman and most also had a holy man who communed with the spirits and was able to produce rain. A really important holy man could control the rising and setting of the sun as well.

Although there was little intercourse between the different islands there was a certain amount of inter-island trade, the large canoes of Santa Cruz travelling hundreds of miles as far as San Cristobal, and the war canoes of Roviana making sporadic raids in search of slaves on Santa Isabel. There are folk tales of something called the Great Peace during which men from the different islands mingled and traded together, but this did not appear to last long.

All men belonged to a clan or tribe, and it was not thought advisable to marry too far out of one's clan as that meant that land-titles and boundaries became involved. In most districts a bride-price of shell money was customary, much of it being spent on the wedding feast.

E

THE SOLOMON ISLANDS

The first recorded voyage of a European into the Pacific Ocean is probably that of the Frenchman Sieur Paulmier de Gonneville. In 1503, this navigator rounded the Cape of Good Hope on a voyage from France to the Indian Ocean, only to be driven off course by a storm. After many days he discovered a large thickly populated island where he stayed for six months. When he returned to Europe he took with him two natives of the land he had discovered. One of them later married his daughter. This land which treated de Gonneville so well has been identified by some as the north-west coast of Australia, but by others as Madagascar or Brazil.

Ten years later, on 26 September 1513, Balboa saw and named the Great South Sea from the coast of Panama, and claimed it on behalf of Spain. In 1520, Hernando Magellan sailed into the South Sea, which he renamed the Pacific Ocean. This voyage was the signal for a number of European expeditions into the Pacific, and navigators and soldiers of fortune braved the unknown ocean in their quest for fame and wealth.

For some time rumours had persisted in Spanish-occupied South America of the existence of a group of islands or even a continent of great wealth somewhere in the South Sea. One Inca legend told of a sea journey supposed to have been made by the fabulous Tupac Yupanqui in which he had discovered two islands, one called Nina-chumpi, or Fire Island, and the other named Hahua-chumpi, or Outer Island. According to the legend, he brought back with him from these islands gold and silver, a throne made of copper, many black slaves, and the skin of an animal like a horse.

One Spaniard who made a study of such stories was Pedro Sarmiento de Gamboa, a soldier and scholar who was destined to become a famous navigator. For seven years Sarmiento made a close study of Peruvian legends about the Pacific islands, and he became convinced that these wealthy islands really existed and that it was possible to fix their bearings. Although he was an extremely gifted man, Sarmiento proved to be cruel, treacherous and disloyal. Not long after his arrival in Peru, a major Spanish possession in the New World, he fell foul of the Inquisition on various charges, including that of practising black magic. Although sentenced to be banished, he got papal permission to remain and eventually persuaded the authorities to launch an expedition in search of the unknown lands which, he claimed, extended from Tierra del Fuego to a latitude of 150° S, and some 600 leagues from Peru. But to Sarmiento's undoubted chagrin he was not put in charge of the expedition. That privilege was granted to Alvaro de Mendana, a young man of twenty-five, nephew of Lope Garcia de Castro, the governor of Peru.

Two ships were provided: the *Los Reyes* (250 tons), and the *Todos Santos* (107 tons), neither of them new. They were stocked with food for the journey and materials for founding a settlement and Mendana was directed to sail for the unknown land, to establish a colony there and 'to convert all infidels to Christianity'.

The two vessels left Calloa in Peru on 19 November 1567. The total complement was 150 men, including 70 soldiers, 4 Franciscan friars and a number of slaves. For the first twenty-six days, because Sarmiento insisted that 'in 15 degrees latitude there were many rich islands', they sailed west-south-west.

Within a month disputes had broken out among the leaders of the expedition. Gallego, the master pilot and an experienced navigator, recommended a more northerly course and, to Sarmiento's mortification, Mendana agreed. For weeks they sailed without sighting land. Food and water ran low. The crew grew mutinous. On 15 January 1568, after sixty-two days at sea, with the remaining supply of water tainted and provisions running dangerously low, they sighted an island now believed to have been Nukufetau, one of the Ellice group. Gallego, judging the tides to be too strong to risk a landing on such an apparently barren outcrop, sailed on. As the navigator later wrote in his log, this led to 'a murmuring among the soldiers, who said that, despite the risk of being lost, they would not leave the island. Being weary of the voyage, they showed great displeasure. . . .'

Seventeen days later both ships narrowly avoided shipwreck on a reef, almost certainly the one near Ontong Java to the north of the Solomons. Immediately after this the vessels were swept away by a cyclone and driven south for six days. On the seventh day the weather cleared and the members of the expedition were overjoyed to see land ahead of them. The date was 7 February 1568. The Spaniards celebrated their deliverance by singing the *Te Deum*, and Mendana named the island Santa Isabel, after the patron saint of the voyage—though for some time the voyagers believed it to be a continent.

At first the local inhabitants were curious but friendly, coming out to meet the ships in their canoes and swarming all over the Spanish vessels. A local chief, Bilebanara, came on board and formally greeted Mendana, exchanging names with the Spaniard, a sign of friendship. Catoira, the chief purser of the fleet and its official chronicler, gives an account of the meeting, noting that the chief

> . . . wore many white and coloured plumes on his head, a head-dress made of them, very white armlets of bone on his wrists, which looked like alabaster, and a small shield on his neck, which they called a tacotaco, and his face was bedaubed with colours. . . . He asked for a cap, offering one of his armlets in return, and with this he appeared satisfied. And the cap being given to him in his canoe, he sent forward some of the Indians, and when they had come on board a negro was playing a flute, and he and the Indians began to perform a dance, the like of which was never seen. The General made him sit down, and asked him his name, and what he called the sun, the moon, the heavens and other things. And he gave them all a name in his language, which is quickly understood, as ours is by them, because they speak distinctly and not affectedly like the people of Peru. They were delighted in storing our words in their memory, and asked us to teach them. . . .

The chief also promised to supply food for the expedition but obviously thought better of his promise when he realised that he was expected to provision 150 hungry men. When, after several days at anchor, no food was forthcoming, Sarmiento was put in charge of an expedition to go ashore and take some. Acting on the advice of the Vicar-General of the Franciscans, Mendana was at pains to impress upon Sarmiento, as he later put it in his journal, that 'He was to take nothing against their will, and to do them no harm, but to pursue his journey'.

Sarmiento was the wrong man to put in charge of such an expedition. Encountering Bilebanara, he tried to seize the chieftain and became involved in a pitched battle with his followers. Men on both sides were wounded in the the fracas, and the Spanish party had to fight its way back to the beach. Not surprisingly relationships with the Santa Isabel people deteriorated. There were scuffles whenever the Europeans sent men ashore from their moored vessels in search of fresh water. Things were not made any easier when Mendana decided to explore the hinterland of the island. Gallego later wrote of this venture :

> At that time the General sent the Master of the Camp, Pedro de Ortega, to see if he could discover what land there was in the interior. He was absent about seven days on this service, and had many skirmishes with the Indians, wherein he burned many temples of the worshippers of snakes, toads, and other insects.

The Spaniards quickly grew disenchanted with the islanders, particularly when it became apparent that there was little wealth to be gathered. One anonymous member of the expedition noted sourly—and inaccurately :

> The Indians of the island of Santa Isabel are idolators; they worship the Devil, who appears to them in the form of a lizard or snake, according to their account. We saw, in some little houses where they pray, many figures of crocodiles and snakes, we even saw some alive in some rooms of the said houses of prayer. The people of this island are brutish, they eat human flesh, and devour people when they can catch them. . . .

73

Meanwhile, Gallego and some of the sailors had been building a small 5-ton brigantine of local timber in which to explore the shallow waters around the islands. They completed their task on 4 April and named the ship *Santiago*. Three days later they set out along the coast of Santa Isabel, leaving the main body of the expedition behind. Then Gallego set a course for some other islands he could see in the distance and eventually they reached a larger island which Ortega the campmaster named after his home village, Guadalcanal. Gallego wrote of their landing on this island :

> Another day, which was the 19th of April, we came to the large island which we had seen, and there was a village of Indians, and a large river. There came out canoes to the brigantine, and some Indians swimming, and some women and boys. We gave them a rope, and drawing it they brought us to land, and when we were near the land they began throwing stones at us, saying 'Mate ! Mate !', meaning to say that they would kill us.

The explorers beat off the attack and sailed back to Santa Isabel to fetch the rest of the expedition to the bay they had named Puerto de la Cruz, on the island of Guadalcanal. Ortega and Gallego had earlier sighted the island of Malaita, but had not gone ashore there.

The Spaniards' sojourn on Guadalcanal was no happier than their stay on Santa Isabel. Again the Europeans were forced to take food by force, angering the islanders, who fought back. The Spaniards retaliated by burning their villages. They made more enemies by capturing islanders and keeping them as hostages and guides, a practice they had begun on Santa Isabel. Even with the food they commandeered ashore, the Spaniards were in a bad way. Mendana, distressed by his failure to establish contact with the natives, gave orders for the two ships to leave Guadalcanal, and they sailed on 13 June.

Gallego had made a number of exploratory voyages in the brigantine and was able to guide Mendana along the coast of Guadalcanal and then down across open seas for seven days until they arrived at the large island they named San Cristobal. No sooner had they landed than the Spaniards again took food by force from a village, driving the inhabitants inland. This meant that there was no chance of coming to terms with the people of that island. Throughout the time the Spaniards stayed on San Cristobal there were skirmishes between the islanders and the soldiers and sailors of the expedition. Many of the Spaniards were ill with fever and other diseases. Their spirits were extremely low. An attempt to find gold on Guadalcanal had come to nothing and there seemed no chance of their establishing a colony in the group. Mendana called a meeting of his pilots and commanders and asked whether they should settle in the islands or return to Peru. By an overwhelming majority the captains elected to sail back to South America. Accordingly the two ships set sail on 11 August 1568, a little over six months after they had first landed in the Solomons.

The homeward journey proved as dangerous and disaster-prone as the rest of the voyage. It was not until 19 December that Mendana sighted lower California after a series of mis-adventures that would have disheartened a less determined man. He was received coldly by the authorities. It was considered that his voyage had done little to advance the cause of Spain. As one official wrote disparagingly to the king of Spain about the islands :

> In my opinion, according to the report that I have received, they were of little importance, although they say that they heard of better lands; for in the course of these discoveries they found no specimens of spices, nor of gold and silver, nor of merchandise, nor of any other source of profit, and all the people were naked savages.

It was at about this time that the unknown islands were first called 'the isles of Solomon' in print. The origin of the name is unknown. It occurs in none of the accounts written by the participants except in that compiled by Sarmiento, which has on the title page 'The Western Islands in the Southern Ocean, commonly called the Isles of Solomon'. Presumably the islands were so called because it was hoped that they would yield as much wealth as that possessed by King Solomon.

This certainly was one of the reasons why Mendana wished to return and found a colony, but it was many years before he realised this ambition. At this time Mendana was out of favour with the governor who succeeded his uncle in Peru; however, he persisted in his efforts and in 1574 a royal decree authorised him to journey to the Solomon Islands, taking with him 500 men—fifty of them to be married with families—together with cattle, horses, pigs and sheep for breeding, and there to found three fortified cities. Mendana was made a marquis and granted the absolute governorship of the colony for two generations, as well as the right to coin gold and silver. But twenty-one years more were to pass before he managed to sail. Political factions in Peru were antagonistic, the presence of Francis Drake and other foreigners in the Pacific discouraged the Spaniards, who were in any case becoming disenchanted with the expense of colonial expansion and exploration. At one time Mendana was even put in prison by his enemies, but was released and with a single-minded devotion continued to plan and plead for a chance to return to the Solomons.

On 5 April 1595, Mendana finally departed, taking with him four ships, more than 300 emigrants, his wife and her three brothers and a chief pilot named Pedro de Quiros. This second expedition was to prove even more disastrous than the first. Supplies of food were insufficient and members of the party were squabbling even before they left Peru. Even Mendana, that most tolerant and optimistic of men, was forced to observe that he was 'very uncertain what would be the end, when the beginning was so disorderly'.

The voyagers landed at a number of islands en route to their destination, including the Marquesas, which they named. Their record everywhere was a disgraceful one of wanton cruelty and destruction. Mendana, dominated by his wife and her relations,

76

was horrified by the needless slaughter of natives but seemed unable to prevent it. Moreover, the expedition did not again find the main Solomons group, though they eventually reached the Santa Cruz islands, hundreds of miles to the east of Mendana's first discoveries. Endeavouring to make the best of a bad job Mendana tried to establish his colony here. It failed. Disease, discontent and hostile islanders combined to cheat Mendana of his dream. He himself died within two months of landing on Santa Cruz and was buried there; the others left and sailed back to Manila in the Philippines, only two ships of the original four completing the homeward journey.

Although the Spaniards' two expeditions to the Solomons were considered a failure by the explorer himself and by his contemporaries, the written accounts he and his colleagues provided do give us a picture of life on the islands, presumably as it had been lived for hundreds of years before the arrival of the first Europeans. They showed that the islanders were competent craftsmen working with tools of stone, building stout canoes and fashioning attractive wooden ornaments; that their houses were soundly constructed of leaf and wood; that agriculture and fishing provided their livelihood; and that they were fierce fighters with spears, clubs and bows and arrows. One member of the first expedition even provided a concise picture of the flora and fauna of the islands :

Certain roots called benaus (taro), a large quantity of yams, smaller roots like potatoes, a great quantity of coconuts, many plantains, wild oranges and limes, sweet cane, wild and in the huts; ginger, wild and in the huts; sweet basil, pigs like those of Castille, quantities of doves, cocks and hens, many other kinds of birds, parrots and macaws, wild geese, mice, good native fruit . . . there are very good eggs, there are little dogs, like the curs of Castille, but they do not all bark, there are bats so large that they measure more than 5ft from the tip of one wing to the tip of another. Throughout the whole of these islands there is not to be found among the Indians a pot, jar or vase of any kind, either made of clay or anything else.

77

Neither is there any kind of metal, gold or silver, pewter, iron nor anything else, except little club-headed stocks of ironstone. Nearly forty men died upon this voyage. God forgive them. Amen!

PEDRO DE QUIROS

Pedro de Quiros succeeded in navigating two ships of Mendana's second expedition back to safety and then spent the next ten years attempting to get backing for the launching of another expedition to find the isles of Solomon and the unknown southern continent. As with Mendana the lure of the islands had a hold upon him, but he was also impelled by the thought of thousands of islanders waiting, as he judged, to be converted to Christianity. No one seemed interested. Quiros even made his way to Europe to secure audiences with the Pope and the king of Spain; his enthusiasm persuaded them both to give approval to his venture. Eventually he also secured the aid of the viceroy of Peru and sailed from Callao with three small ships on 21 December 1605.

Quiros experienced as much trouble with his subordinates as Mendana had done. Both his second-in-command, Torres, and his chief pilot, Bilboa, were constantly bickering. Quiros allowed himself to be persuaded by the pilot to change course. It seems now that if they had proceeded on their original way they might well have discovered New Zealand. As it was, surviving the inevitable shortages of food and water and the discontent of the crew, they passed the Cook Islands and then on 7 April 1606 sighted Taumako in the Duff group in the eastern Solomons.

Quiros had hoped to land at Santa Cruz, and although he did not know it Taumako was only a day's sail away. At first the men of the Duffs were truculent, but Quiros ordered a musket to be fired and this put an end to any contemplated resistance. The friars on board went ashore and said Mass. Quiros, a deeply religious man, was tempted to stay and convert the natives. He would also have liked to have revisited Santa Cruz, but the great aim of his expedition was to discover the huge unknown continent thought to exist somewhere in the Pacific. Accordingly on

18 April, he hauled up his anchors and sailed away from the Solomons never to return. On this expedition he reached the New Hebrides and there founded a bizarre religious colony which he termed New Jerusalem. The colony was a failure and Quiros returned ignominiously to Peru.

RE-DISCOVERY

Throughout the seventeenth century there are records of only two European vessels approaching the Solomons. Both were Dutch, because trading ships from Holland were beginning to follow the Spanish and English into the Pacific, and in each case the island approached and sighted was Ontong Java, the Polynesian outlier to the north of the main group. The Amsterdam merchant adventurer Le Maire is believed to have sighted the islands in 1616 and his better-known compatriot Abel Tasman also saw the group and named it in 1643. The word Ontong is thought to be derived from the Malay *untung*, which means luck. J. C. Beaglehole is of the opinion that Tasman meant the name to signify Java luck, or good fortune.

Neither Le Maire nor Tasman is recorded as having landed at Ontong Java, although the latter put an illustration of the group of islands in his journal. Thus in effect the Solomons were not visited by Europeans for over 160 years after Quiros paid his fleeting visit to Taumako in the Duffs. In his introduction to the English version of Mendana's narrative, Lord Amherst makes some interesting points about this disappearance of the Solomons from European view.

The main cause seems to have been the vagaries of mapmakers of the time, allied to the unavailability of original sources. The first printed account of Mendana's discovery appeared briefly in Antonio Herrers's *Description de las Indias Occidentales,* which was published in Madrid in 1601. This map, and the facts accompanying it, were derived from hearsay and were grossly inaccurate. A more reliable account was published twelve years later, in 1613, by Figueroa (*Hechos de Don Garcia Hurtado de Mendoza, Quarto Marques de Canete, por el Doctor Christoval Suarez de Figueroa*, Madrid) but the narratives of members of Mendana's expeditions languished in the archives of the Indies in Spain and later inaccuracies in maps and descriptions went unchecked and uncorrected. Thanks to Mendana the Solomons were first approximately marked on maps in 1587. Less than sixty years later in Dudley's *Arcano del Mare* of 1646 they are identified with the Marquesas. At the beginning of the eighteenth century Delisle has them farther west, Danville does not show them at all, and Dalrymple in 1790 confuses them with New Britain.

It was not until the second half of the eighteenth century that a European again visited the Solomons. By this time the Pacific was no longer quite the unknown ocean it once had been. The power of the Spanish had waned, but England and Holland, the two major seafaring nations of the period, were doggedly pushing their way across the South Sea. By the middle of the seventeenth century the Dutch had already crossed the ocean a dozen times, with men of the calibre of Van Noort, Spielberg, Schouten and Le Maire commanding their vessels in the wake of Britain's Drake, while Tasman had sailed round Australia and passed both Fiji and Tonga. After the trade-hunting Dutch came the buccaneering British. Sea-dogs like Dampier, Cavendish and Woods-Rogers looted Spanish settlements on the coast of America and went in search of the Spanish treasure galleons sailing from Manila. In the course of their piratical endeavours these Britons accomplished amazing feats of seamanship—Dampier twice visited unknown Australia—but they were interested mainly in booty, not in exploration.

Dutch traders and British buccaneers gave way to the era of scientific exploration and discovery, culminating in the three fantastic voyages of Captain James Cook between 1768 and 1779. All the voyages of this period were official government ventures to discover new lands or to make scientific explorations.

One such expedition was undertaken by Captain Philip Carteret in the sloop HMS *Swallow*. Carteret's task was to accompany Captain Samuel Wallis in the frigate *Dolphin* in an attempt to find the unknown southern continent. The two ships left Plymouth in August 1766, and in April of the following year the vessels became separated in bad weather while approaching the Straits of Magellan and did not again find one another. Carteret, his vessel leaking and constantly threatening to founder, passed round the tip of South America and beat across the Pacific. Hounded by bad weather, Carteret discovered and named the tiny outcrop of Pitcairn Island and then much later the Tuamotus.

By now Carteret's vessel was in a dreadful state and her crew scarcely better. The masts had rotted and threatened to come down at any moment, and scurvy was rampant on board. Staggering blindly across the Pacific, desperately looking for an island which would provide fresh water and vegetables, the captain decided to try for Mendana's Solomon Islands. For days he searched, using the faulty charts of the period. Finding no sign of the group at the latitude described in his maps, he almost despaired, confiding to his log that 'if there were any such islands, their situation was erroneously laid down'.

Then Ndeni, the major island in the Santa Cruz group was discovered. It was so far from the spot marked on the map that Carteret refused to believe that he had stumbled across the Solmons, and named the group Queen Charlotte's Islands. Greatly cheered, the captain sent a boat ashore to explore and look for food and water. When the members of the landing party returned they reported that the island was wild and mountainous and that they had spotted a number of naked savages who had fled from them. The following day another group of sailors went ashore and insulted the local inhabitants by cutting down a coconut tree. The islanders attacked the sailors with bows and arrows, wounding a number of them. Carteret determined to leave Santa Cruz as soon as possible. While his vessel was being repaired he turned her guns on the shore to repel any attacks. Eventually the *Swallow* was able to leave the harbour.

Before quitting the Solomons, Carteret saw the island of Malaita and a few of the smaller islands, but made no attempt to land on any of them. Passing through the western Solomons he reached New Britain and then Batavia where he had his ship repaired before heading for South Africa and then England. On his way home he encountered and exchanged courtesies with a French vessel, the *Boudeuse*, commanded by the Chevalier de Bougainville. A charming picture has been handed on of the unkempt and bedraggled Englishman exchanging polite conversation with the impeccable French captain who was later to become famous as the discoverer of more of the Solomon group.

Louis de Bougainville, a former aide-de-camp of Montcalm who had lost Quebec and Canada to General Wolfe, had been commissioned by his government to make a voyage of discovery round the world. He sailed in the *Boudeuse*, accompanied by a store-ship, the *Etoile*, in 1766. Rounding the Straits of Magellan he landed at Tahiti, visited Samoa and the New Hebrides and then headed south. At the Great Barrier Reef he turned back without seeing Australia and made north, hoping to reach New Britain. Instead he passed through the western Solomons. The French captain was not sure of his position but he named the islands of Buka and Bougainville. He also discovered and named Choiseul and off the coast of this island he was attacked by ten canoes full of armed islanders. Two of the canoes were captured by the French and the rest driven off. The members of the expedition were impressed by the workmanship and carvings on the canoes but were not so taken by the jawbone of a man they found in the bottom of one of them.

Bougainville could see that the occupants of the islands were brave and warlike; it was quite common for individual canoes to try and attack the European vessel by discharging arrows at it. The captain mapped the shores of the islands as he sailed past but did not linger for any great length of time in these waters.

He made his way to New Britain and then to Batavia before returning to France : although he had learned little about the isles of Solomon he had mapped the western area of the group. Now that a trail had been blazed other navigators began to visit the Solomons. In 1769 Surville, a Frenchman, landed at Santa Isabel and toured the surrounding islands, ominously naming them Terre des Arsacides (Land of Assassins). He was followed in 1781 by the Spaniard Maurelle.

Buache, a Frenchman, was convinced by his study of all the available accounts, that the Solomons must lie within twelve and a half degrees of longitude somewhere between Santa Cruz and New Guinea, and in 1781 put forward his theory that the islands seen by Bougainville and Surville were a part of the Solomon group. Not everyone agreed with him; both Dalrymple and Cook in Great Britain were convinced that the Solomon islands Mendana had discovered were the islands of New Britain. The French decided to put Buache's theory to the test. In 1786 they instructed one of their Pacific explorers, La Pérouse, to follow Buache's charts and see if they did bring him to the Solomons. Obediently La Pérouse left France with two frigates, *Boussole* and *Astrolabe*. Two years later he reached Australia after a voyage which had taken in the Philippines and Samoa among other islands. The Frenchman arrived at Botany Bay in New South Wales only a few days after Governor Arthur Phillip's first fleet had arrived at the new colony with the first consignment of convicts and their guards. Phillip was engrossed in his plans to transfer the colony to a new site, the later Sydney Harbour area, and deputed his second-in-command, Captain John Hunter, to pay the courtesy visit to the French vessels.

La Pérouse made a favourable impression on the British with his charm and courtesy. In February he left New South Wales to follow the route laid down by the French authorities. Neither he nor his crew were ever seen again.

The loss of the two vessels caused great distress in France and efforts were made to launch an expedition to look for the missing ships. While this operation was being organised, more vessels were sailing through the Solomon seas. It was shortly after the disappearance of *Boussole* and *Astrolabe* that John Shortland in command of the *Alexander* and *Friendship* saw the islands that were to bear his name. Shortland went ashore at the island of Simbo and also named New Georgia. Two years later, Captain Wilkinson certainly named Indispensable Strait and Indispensable Reef in the vicinity of these islands, after his ship *Indispensable*. In 1790 Captain Ball sailed along the coasts of Guadalcanal and San Cristobal and passed the Russells. The next year, 1791, John Hunter also saw the Solomons. Now that the colony in New South Wales was established, the Solomon Islands were less off the beaten track. Hunter saw Sikaiana and its adjoining islands and called them the Stewart Islands. He also landed on Tasman's atoll, Ontong Java, where he found the inhabitants friendly and renamed the group Lord Howe; today the islands bear both names.

By 1791 the French expedition to search for the missing La Pérouse was ready, consisting of two ships, the *Recherche* and the *Espérance* under the overall command of Admiral Antoine-Raymond-Joseph d'Entrecasteaux. The vessels sailed on 28 September with instructions to retrace the route thought to have been followed by La Pérouse after he had left Botany Bay. Eventually the French admiral reached the Santa Cruz group, naming the uncharted island of Recherche, later to be known as Utupua. No wreckage was observed but d'Entrecasteaux took care to map the islands of the area and then sailed on past the shores of San Cristobal, Ulawa, Guadalcanal and New Georgia. The expedition suffered badly from scurvy and other diseases and the admiral himself died before the ships returned, unsuccessful, to France.

Thirty years later the wreckage, or what was believed to be the wreckage, of La Pérouse's ships, was discovered off the island of Vanikolo in the Santa Cruz group. Local inhabitants later told a visiting ship that some of the sailors from the expedition had

Page 85 (above) Malaita. Langa Langa Lagoon, surf breaking far left; (below) Guadalcanal 'Red Beach' today with no sign of war, but where the US marines landed, 7 August 1942

Page 86 (above) Welcoming party attired as traditional 'wild men' to celebrate the opening of a clinic on Savo Island; (below) Polynesian musical interlude round a beached canoe on Bellona

been saved but that they had built themselves another ship and sailed away in it, presumably to their deaths.

So, by the end of the eighteenth century visitors from the outside world were beginning once again to journey to the Solomons. As Lord Amherst writes :

> In the history of travel there is probably no other instance of the veil being lifted for a brief moment to afford a glimpse of the life of an isolated island race, and then dropped again for nigh three centuries, during which no ripple came from the outer world to disturb the silent backwater.

Certainly the accounts given by the first travellers to revisit the group indicate that the way of life of the Solomon Islanders had continued virtually unchanged during the silent centuries. Head-hunting and cannibalism were still practised. The islanders were still smearing their hair with lime to lighten its colour, wearing cockatoo feathers and shell bracelets, playing pan pipes and blowing conch shells. They were still chewing betel-nut and using shell money, decorating their custom houses with carvings of reptiles and the bones of animals. Only in incidentals had there been any changes. The warriors of Santa Isabel appeared to have given up the use of the heavy and powerful longbow in favour of the spear, and areas of Guadalcanal and Santa Isabel which the Spaniards had reported as being heavily populated were now less so.

Hundreds of years of immunity from European civilisation had helped to preserve the traditions and customs of the Solomon Islands. With the dawning of the nineteenth century this immunity came to an end. The Solomon Islands were never to become widely known, but never again were they to be completely isolated from the world outside.

F

4 VISITORS AND SETTLERS

ALTHOUGH the Solomons, like most of the Pacific islands, had been mapped by the end of the eighteenth century there was no immediate rush of visitors from the world outside. For quite a few years the only Europeans to approach the islands were those sailors making their way to or from Australia. In 1797 the missionary ship *Duff*, famed for taking the first evangelists from the old world to the South Seas, passed and named the Duff Islands which contained the village of Taumako previously visited by Quiros in 1606. No other vessel is reported to have approached the group until the ship *Hunter* landed, at their own request, three strangers at the outer island of Tikopia, sailing away and leaving them there. The three castaways were a German doctor called Buckhardt, his Fijian wife and a Lascar seaman. The year of their arrival is given as 1813.

No one knows why these three people chose to be left on this tiny island, but they seem to have been the first outsiders to have attempted to settle in the Solomons since the days of Mendana. The ship which put them ashore was a sandalwood trader and one of the officers on board was Peter Dillon, later a famous navigator in the Pacific. Thirteen years later Dillon called again at Tikopia to find the three people still there, living perfectly happily. The Lascar seems to have done a certain amount of travelling by canoe for he showed Dillon a sword handle and other European articles which he said had been found at Vanikolo, another island in the area. Dillon later reported this, and in 1828 a French expedition under Dumont d'Urville arrived at

Vanikolo in search of any survivors of La Pérouse's expedition, as it was thought that the sword handle must have belonged to one of his officers.

By 1830 whalers from America, Australia and Europe were hunting in Solomon waters and occasionally landing at the islands for food and water and to effect repairs. The latter were often necessary for storms were frequent and the reefs treacherous. Not every vessel succeeded in avoiding disaster of this kind, and survivors of a wreck often found themselves in further difficulties. In 1829 there were reports of twenty shipwrecked whalers being imprisoned and then eaten by the islanders on Malaita. In other parts of the group white men were more fortunate. In an epic voyage from Tasmania, eleven escaped convicts led by a man called Stewart made their way in a stolen boat past Tonga, New Caledonia and the New Hebrides and after two years reached Tikopia where the inhabitants allowed them to settle.

Only occasionally is the curtain lifted in this fashion to allow a glimpse of life in the Solomons in the early decades of the nineteenth century. There can be little doubt that an increasing number of vessels were visiting the islands, first the whalers, then sandalwood traders and later trading ships of other kinds. Now and again a white man stayed behind when his ship left, cast away by his comrades or deserting from the rigorous discipline of maritime life. His fate depended much upon the area: a European on Malaita or Guadalcanal would have little chance of survival, but in the west he might be accepted and even given a little land and a wife. The sailors from La Pérouse's expedition seem to have survived on Vanikolo for some years, and in 1844 Captain Cheyne in the brig *Naiad* put in at Simbo and found three Englishmen living there, and at Sikaiana also he came across two more beachcombers.

None of the beachcombers left behind written accounts of the native way of life as they found it, and many years were to pass before the missionaries arrived and began to write down what

89

they saw around them. Neither did the Solomons receive as many visitors as other island groups in the South Pacific, partly due to their remoteness, but also to the forbidding stories of hostility and cannibalism which came out of the dark islands. Vessels in search of turtle shells and the Chinese delicacy known as bêche de mer did trade cautiously in the Solomons but took care to confine their activities to the more hospitable shores of New Georgia and Sikaiana.

By 1840 trading schooners and brigs from Sydney were making their way to the Solomons in increasing number, having exploited and exhausted the islands nearer Australia. It was also a two-way traffic. When whalers and traders putting in at the islands were short-handed due to sickness and desertion, islanders were given the chance of signing on. Some of them accepted the opportunity and in this way travelled to other island groups and even to New South Wales, where four men of San Cristobal are recorded as having worked as boatmen in Sydney Harbour. These were not the first Solomon Islanders to go overseas—Mendana had taken some back to Peru with him after his first voyage, and in 1769 de Surville had kidnapped Lova Saregua from Santa Isabel and put him on display in France.

It appears that the whalers got on well enough with the islanders, but the sandalwood traders, their name a byword for cruelty and avarice, were a different story. In New Caledonia and the New Hebrides they forced their way ashore and slaughtered hundreds of islanders in their search for the sweet-smelling wood so prized by the Chinese as incense. When they came to the Solomons it was not for wood but to buy turtle shell (known as tortoise shell), pearl shell and pigs to exchange with the New Hebrideans for sandalwood. They gave the islanders much appreciated tools of steel and iron, but their hard bargaining and unscrupulous ways antagonised many and there were a number of pitched battles between sailors and islanders. By the 1840s the Solomons were notorious as the home of savage fighters who did not take kindly to strangers. But some traders, those who proved themselves to be honest, were accepted, and their knives of steel soon replaced the old stone tools.

For a time missionaries were slow to come to the Solomons. Most of the other islands in the Pacific were evangelised before the attention of the churches was turned once again to the Solomons. The first missionary attempt was made by the Catholics, a group from the Society of Mary under Bishop Jean-Baptiste Epalle landing on Santa Isabel in 1845.

The vicariates of Micronesia and Melanesia had been formed in 1844 and Epalle had been consecrated as bishop in charge. He had earlier been in New Zealand and was convinced that Melanesia should be evangelised at once before the traders and seamen corrupted it as they had corrupted the Polynesian islands to the east. With seven priests and six brothers he reached Sydney in June 1845, and set out to find out as much as he could about the Solomons which, being the remotest of the Melanesian islands, he decided had most need of the services of the Marists.

There was little to discover about the group. Makira Harbour on San Cristobal was fairly well known as the place where whalers careened their vessels, and Santa Isabel was thought to have good harbours and anchorages. Other reports, such as they were, were not encouraging. The Solomon Islanders were vigorous and hard working, skilled agriculturists but much more dour than the happy-go-lucky Polynesians, savage fighters, suspicious of strangers and inclined to head-hunting and cannibalism. The Melanesians of the neighbouring New Hebrides had, only six years before, murdered John Williams and a colleague from the London Missionary Society.

Epalle was convinced that the Solomons were the place for him : there were no missionaries of other faiths there, so the cry could not go up that the Catholics were forcing their way into the territory of the London Missionary Society or the Methodists or other denominations then active in the Pacific. Santa Isabel was chosen as the site of his first Marist mission. In December Epalle and his associates anchored in Astrolabe Harbour in Thousand Ships Bay. The local inhabitants were friendly at first and eager to trade for the iron and steel axes and knives the missionaries had brought with them. Their lack of shyness led Epalle to conclude that the Isabel people were not unaccustomed to the sight of European traders.

The people of Astrolabe Harbour warned Bishop Epalle not to go beyond Maunga Point at the mouth of the harbour. If he did, they said he would encounter their enemies who would automatically be hostile to the Europeans as they had been seen trading with the Astrolabe Harbour people.

Bishop Epalle dismissed the warnings. On 16 December, he sailed his ship past the point and went ashore in the ship's boat with some of his colleagues. Over sixty canoes came out to escort the boat, and another mob of people were drawn up upon the sands, waiting for Epalle to land. Two sailors remained to guard the boat while the bishop and one priest and a lay brother went up the beach, followed by the mate and two other sailors who for some reason, perhaps at the bishop's command, left their rifles in the ship's boat.

Epalle tried to converse with some of the islanders and gave a small axe to a young man who appeared to be their leader, but the latter treated all overtures with contempt. Another islander offered the bishop two lemons, one of them partly eaten, in exchange for his episcopal ring. When the bishop refused the islanders began jostling the strangers. The Europeans tried to make their way back to the boat and this seemed to be the signal for an attack. The bishop was struck on the head from behind by an axe and fell. The others managed to drag him back to the boat and got him on board the mission ship. He died three days later.

Another father took over the Santa Isabel mission and the Catholics were allowed to buy land in another district, but the mission was not a success. Three more missionaries were killed by the local people and another died. The mission was finally abandoned in 1852 and it was over forty years before the Catholics returned to the Solomons. One small mission was started at Tikopia in the east, but when a ship put in at the island a year or two later there was no sign of the priests who had been put ashore there and vanished.

TRADERS AND SLAVERS

Only six years after the martyrdom of Bishop Epalle, a trader was murdered at Wanderer Bay on Guadalcanal. The murdered man was Benjamin Boyd, one of the most unusual of all the eccentric characters about in the mid-nineteenth century.

Boyd had done a bit of everything in his time, including founding the Royal Australian Bank and the Australian Wool Company, building a township in New South Wales to supply whalers with supplies, and importing some of the first Pacific Islanders into Australia for the purpose of looking after his sheep. The sixty-five natives brought in from the Loyalty Islands and the New Hebrides were the first indentured islanders to be introduced into Australia. It was the beginning of the dark ages in the islands of the South Pacific. Impressed by Boyd's method of obtaining cheap labour, other merchants sent vessels to the islands on what were little more than slaving expeditions. With the ending of the transportation of convicts from the old world the farmers and settlers of the outback needed farm hands : the islands were to provide them. In order to obtain a sufficient supply of islanders the crews of ships would sometimes kidnap the chief of an area and hold him to ransom until enough of his followers had surrendered themselves and agreed to go to Australia. All sorts of ruses and stratagems were employed in the Solomons and elsewhere to round up labourers, and a tremendous wave of anti-European feeling swept the Pacific. No white man was safe, missionaries and traders were regarded as no better than the slave traders, and many were murdered.

93

Some of the islanders imported into Australia were well enough treated and returned after the period of their indentures—usually three to five years—with a supply of steel and iron tools and an enhanced reputation as 'big men', who had been overseas and were now wealthy. Others were less fortunate and worked in abysmal conditions, constantly abused and beaten. The white labourers hated the islanders. Writing to the London *Times* in 1847 Mark Boyd, the brother of Benjamin, was most aggrieved about this :

> Detached parties of them [the islanders] were at first sent to stations in the interior, from one of which, after having actively and usefully assisted in the washing of 10,000 sheep, they were summarily driven by those who are colonially termed 'the old hands' and who, anxious to maintain the exorbitant rate of wages exacted for pastoral labour, regarded the newcomers with jealousy. Similar treatment from the Europeans in other quarters drove a further portion of them to Sydney.

The European labourers obviously saw that with the introduction of imported slave labour their livelihoods were at stake. There was little that they could do about it. Over the next fifty years thousands of the 'kanaka' labourers were to be imported into Australia. Ironically, Boyd did not make the vast fortune out of his idea that he probably expected. By 1851, his business ventures crumbling, beset on all sides by lawsuits, Boyd decided that discretion was the better part of valour and put to sea in his yacht, the *Wanderer*. After an unsuccessful foray into the California gold fields, he decided to try his luck in the South Pacific. Boyd's fertile mind was now teeming with ideas of taking over one of the islands and turning it into his own kingdom, perhaps importing sheep on a large scale and encouraging other Europeans to join him later.

Unfortunately, the first island he decided to investigate for these purposes was Guadalcanal in the Solomons. On 15 October Boyd went ashore at a place later named Wanderer Bay after his ship. He intended to shoot game and took a native boy with him to carry his gun. When Boyd had not returned by late afternoon a search party went ashore to look for him, and was attacked by a band of islanders but managed to regain the ship's boat and pull back to the *Wanderer*. No sooner had they done so than a fleet of war canoes swept round the point, heading for the ship. A blast from the *Wanderer*'s cannon destroyed one of the war canoes and the rest turned and fled. Later a further effort was made to find Boyd, but it was unsuccessful and the *Wanderer* left the area.

Boyd had been a well-known figure in the Pacific and the report of his death caused a stir, the Solomons getting an even worse reputation for ferocity. A number of ships visited Guadalcanal in an effort to find Boyd's body, all without success. In 1853 HMS *Serpent* searched the area, and a year later HMS *Herald* under Captain Denham made an official investigation. The only result of these enquiries was that a convict on board the *Herald*, one Dennis Griffith, managed to escape and run into the bush at Wanderer Bay. He was never heard of again.

Other beachcombers continued to settle. In 1860 three were known to be living on San Cristobal, one of them being Frederick Bradford, former mate of the whaler *Oynx*. Some of these beachcombers acted as local agents for the traders who were beginning to set up stores on a number of the islands. On the side, these men were not above joining in local feuds if they were well enough paid, bringing their muskets to the aid of any chief who could meet their price. Their existence was a precarious one, however, and these soldiers of fortune never knew when their allies among the islanders would turn against them.

After tools and nails, muskets and rum were the most highly favoured items of trade among the islanders. The decline of the whaling industry was balanced by an increasing demand for coconut oil and copra, and the traders were quick to adapt to the new circumstances. With the advent of Australian vessels looking for labourers in the islands the position of the traders became less tenable and then when the notorious 'blackbirding' began in

95

Melanesia, it was every man for himself as far as expatriates were concerned.

'Blackbirding' was the name given to the practice of kidnapping islanders and taking them off to work as slave labour overseas. It had begun in a small way with Benjamin Boyd and his fellows, but it attained the status of almost a major industry with the growth of the sugar plantations of Queensland and Fiji. This took place between 1860 and 1865 and for over twenty years there was a constant demand for native labour to toil under the sun cutting sugar cane. The Solomon islands became the target of the slave-trading vessels, whose captains and agents were paid by the head for each labourer brought back to Fiji or Queensland.

Some islanders volunteered to make the journey, but this supply of volunteer labour soon dried up and the blackbirding vessels resorted to other methods. Sometimes the captains would bribe district chieftains with rifles and other goods to send the young men of the area on board the ships. At other times raiding parties would go ashore. Here is an account of a typical blackbirding raid, as seen by an islander :

> Many months ago a big boat with white sails anchored off the beach of Owa Raka. There were many white men on board and also many black men whom they had for the most part captured from other islands. The sailing ship put out many small boats in which white men sat with big thunder-sticks. The little boats approached the reef and the white men tried to catch a number of our people who were fishing with hooks and spears there. Our people saw the danger and ran away. They jumped from rock to rock and swam through the high breakers. The white men tried to cut off their retreat and succeeded in surrounding ten of them. When they saw that there was no escape they began to defend themselves. But it was a very unequal fight. Many of the strangers, who were all well armed, fell at a time on one of our men, who had only their fishing spears with them. Six of them were killed in this way and the tide carried their dead bodies out to the unending water. Four fell into the hands of the enemy. They were bound so that

the sharp cords cut deep into their flesh, and sand and stones were stuffed into their mouths to stop their screaming.

Malaita was a favourite calling point for the blackbirders. Originally a number of Malaita men, short of land as usual, had volunteered for the sugar plantations. There was a great deal of fighting when the bush people made their way to the coast to sign on the blackbirding ships and the occupants of the salt-water areas killed a number of them. Those that survived and reached Australia and Fiji made reputations as good workers. The recruiting vessels came back to Malaita for more workers. Finding no volunteers, they would drop stones into the bottoms of canoes, tumbling the occupants into the water and then fish them out and imprison them in dreadful conditions below deck until a full complement of labourers had been gathered.

Before long the islanders learned to trust no one. They were waiting on the shores if a boat put ashore from a foreign ship and their warriors would kill all the white occupants of such vessels.

THE MISSIONS

By the middle years of the century missionaries were again making their way to the Solomons to try to bring Christianity to the troubled shores of the dark islands. In 1850 the Australasian Board of Missions was formed. It was headed by the Anglican Bishop of New Zealand, George Augustus Selwyn. Its purpose was to support a Christian Mission to Melanesia. Selwyn had been Bishop of New Zealand for some years and was a vigorous and controversial figure. Determined and energetic, this former rowing blue travelled across great tracts of unknown country in New Zealand, doing a great deal for the Maoris but antagonising members of his own church and causing a rift with the Methodists because of his unwillingness to compromise.

In the early years of his work in New Zealand the bishop had been too busy to spare the time to visit the isles of Melanesia which came within his jurisdiction, but in 1851 he sailed to the

97

Solomons, the first of a number of such voyages. In four years he visited over fifty islands of Melanesia, making friends with the people and taking young men of the islands back with him to New Zealand for training as catechists. Selwyn saw that there was a great deal of work to be done in Melanesia and that he needed a dedicated man who would concentrate solely on the work in the islands. Accordingly he returned to England to find such a man.

He met a young curate, John Coleridge Patteson, the son of a judge, a former captain of cricket at Eton and an Oxford graduate. Patteson, a large, athletic man, had heard Selwyn preach before his departure for New Zealand many years previously and had been much impressed by the young bishop's words. Now that Selwyn was looking for someone to assist him Patteson was convinced that he had a vocation to go to the Pacific. He was accepted and the two of them sailed for New Zealand.

In 1856 Bishop Selwyn took Patteson with him on his first trip to the Solomons. The main object of the voyage was to collect boys from the islands and take them to a school in New Zealand for part of the year and then to return them to their homes. The first island visited by the priests was Rennell, and it is possible that they were the first white men to land there. They were greeted with enthusiasm by the friendly Polynesians who swarmed all over the mission ship. Many of the islanders spent the night on board, singing the kaka, the song of love.

The first voyage of Patteson's was a great success. Now and again he came across a grim reminder of local customs; on San Cristobal, for example, he and Selwyn were taken to a building in which there were twenty-eight skulls gathered by the islanders on head-hunting expeditions. They visited Guadalcanal, Malaita and the Santa Cruz islands before returning to New Zealand. Here Patteson began teaching Melanesian boys at the Anglican school at Kohimarama, near Auckland. He grew very fond of his young charges and was popular with them. At the end of the year he sailed back to the Solomons to return his pupils to their homes, the expectation being that these boys would spread the word of God among their own people.

It was the first of many such voyages for Patteson. In 1857 he called at sixty-six islands, made eighty-one landings and brought away thirty-five pupils. It was proof of his personality that the dour islanders allowed their children to go with the young priest, although Patteson was liberal with his presents of axes and knives, often swimming ashore when the weather was too rough for a ship's boat to venture over the reef.

In 1861 Patteson was consecrated first Bishop of Melanesia. He was thirty-four years old and was to spend the next ten years of his life in the islands. He kept on with his school, transferring it to Norfolk Islands, and constantly brought boys from the New Hebrides and Solomons to be educated there. For a time it looked as if his personality and energy might be enough to convert thousands of islanders, but the work of the blackbirders put an end to that. The raids of the slave traders undid all the good work of Patteson and his fellow missionaries. Some of the blackbirders even pretended to be missionaries, winning the trust of the islanders and then falling upon them.

In turn the islanders grew to distrust the missionaries. In 1864 Patteson was attacked at Santa Cruz. Two of his colleagues, Edwin Nobbs and Fisher Young, were killed and the bishop was lucky to escape with his life. Seven years later he too was murdered. He had set out on yet another missionary journey to the Melanesian islanders. Everywhere he found that the labour-recruiting vessel had been before him. At Whitsuntide Island many men had been carried off by a 'thief ship'; almost every man had been taken from Merlav and the missionaries estimated that almost half the population of the Banks Islands over the age of ten had been kidnapped. In the Floridas fifty men had gone on board a vessel to trade. They had all been carried off to Queensland. Sailors on board the vessel had smashed the canoes attempting to give chase by hurling rocks down at them.

THE SOLOMON ISLANDS

On the morning of 20 September 1871, Bishop Patteson went ashore at the tiny island of Nukapu in the Santa Cruz group. His companions begged him not to go, but Patteson was adamant. The chief was a friend of his, he insisted, they had even exchanged names on a previous visit. But the thief ships had visited the island since that time. Five boys had been seized and taken off to Fiji by a man impersonating the bishop. As Patteson landed he was followed to the shelter of a canoe house and murdered by the uncle of one of the kidnapped boys. Two other missionaries were also killed. Patteson's body was recovered and buried at sea.

The death of the bishop caused a storm of indignation in Great Britain and Australia and led to sterner methods being taken to put down the worse excesss of the labour-recruiting trade. A man of war shelled Nukapu as a reprisal for the murder, five schooners were added to the Australian Squadron of the Royal Navy to help suppress blackbirding, and in the same year, 1872, the Imperial Pacific Islanders Protection Act, amended three years later, gave more protection to islanders. The recruitment of labourers for the Australian sugar fields was to go on for more than thirty years—the last 2,000 islanders returned from Queensland in 1906—but after the death of Patteson the outright abduction of natives became less blatant.

The death of Patteson did not deter the Melanesian Mission. Other missionaries followed the murdered bishop, including the son of George Selwyn, who became Bishop of Melanesia. In 1875, the year in which Commander Goodenough and two sailors were speared on Santa Cruz and later died of tetanus, the Reverend Alfred Penny began ten years' missionary work on Santa Isabel. Penny was to be the first of a long line of Anglican priest-scholars which included Ivens, Codrington and Fox. These missionaries, and others like them, studied the way of life of the people with whom they were living and compiled dictionaries and grammars of their languages, bringing literacy to the islands.

100

Other missions reached the Solomons. After the Anglicans came the Catholics, for the second time, when the Marists returned under Bishop Vidal and opened a mission station on Rua Sura in 1898. The South Seas Evangelical Church and the Methodists did not arrive until the first decade of the twentieth century, and their story properly belongs in that era.

LAW AND ORDER

European law and order were slow of establishment in the Solomons. After the martyrdom of Bishop Patteson in 1871 and the slaughter of Commander Goodenough and his companions in 1875, other outbreaks of violence continued to take place in the islands, variously described as acts of self-defence by the islanders or wanton examples of pagan savagery, according to which point of view was taken. In 1876 all but two of the crew of the *Dancing Wave* were massacred when attempting to 'recruit' pearl divers from Nggela. The two survivors were rescued by Captain Woodhouse in the *Sydney*.

By this time a number of Europeans were striving to earn a living in the Solomons. Among them were Lars Nielsen, Frank Wickham and Stanley Bateman, all of whom are mentioned often in the logs of ships putting in to the islands. All these men were traders, dealing mainly in copra, exchanging some 40lb of tobacco, valued at £3, for each ton of copra produced, although other trade goods like knives and axes were acceptable in place of tobacco. Few of these traders made vast fortunes out of their dealings; their annual profit would be about £300, and for the risks they ran it was not a vast sum. In 1878 a trader gathering copra at Ugi was murdered. In reply the village was burnt by sailors from HMS *Beagle*. Two years later Lieutenant Bower and three of the crew of HMS *Sandfly* surveying the waters of the Solomons were murdered on Nggela. At about this time Gorai, the leading chief of the Shortlands, negotiated with labour recruiters for a supply of weapons in exchange for labourers, a practice which was copied by Kwaisulia, a chief on Malaita. Supplies of rifles made each chief almost invincible.

Plainly something had to be done to protect British nationals in the area, and in 1877 a Western Pacific Order in Council extended British law to its subjects in the Solomons. British interest in the Solomons was intensified when it was realised that Germany was beginning to join the race for Pacific possessions. Britain was not sure that it wanted the Solomons, especially when in 1886 the recruiting vessel *Young Dick* was attacked at Siner- ango on Malaita and most of its crew murdered, but the Foreign Office did not want Germany to spread its net too wide in the South Pacific. In 1886, after some negotiations, Britain and Germany made a joint declaration of their areas of interest in the group. Britain took the south Solomons while Germany accepted the northern islands of Bougainville, Buka, Choiseul and Santa Isabel as its sphere of influence. Germany raised its flag on Choiseul but reserved most of its attention for New Guinea. Great Britain, on the other hand, was now actively en- gaged in the southern Solomons, even if only on punitive raids.

The British government could not have been overjoyed by its latest acquisition. In 1889 Kwaisulia, the Malaita chieftain in possession of rifles and a thousand warriors, found himself en- gaged in a war with the neighbouring Manaoba people. In order to secure assistance the enterprising chief asked to be annexed by Fiji. No sooner had this been refused than Howard, a trader at Ugi, was murdered by Malaita men. At the same time the head- hunting raids of the Roviana warriors reached a new peak and Captain Davies was sent in HMS *Royalist* to suppress the head- hunting as firmly as possible. This he accomplished by shelling and burning every village in the Roviana Lagoon, destroying an estimated 400 houses and 150 canoes. He also razed a fortress on Roviana Island.

Not even the most sanguine British official could have been pleased with the situation in the Solomons. Something had to be done to regularise the position. In 1893 a British protectorate was

Page 103 Traditional dances: (above) a giant, armed with a spear, is killed by a warrior brandishing an Isabel spear in Santa Isabel dance; (below) costume dance at Guadalcanal to celebrate opening of airstrip at Avu Avu

Page 104 Missions: *(above)* Wango harbour, San Cristoval, where the celebrated missionary, Dr C. E. Fox lived for many years, studying language and customs; *(below)* Seventh Day Adventist mission station at Viru harbour, New Georgia

proclaimed over the southern Solomons by Captain Gibson in HMS *Curacao*, sailing under sealed orders. The area included consisted of New Georgia, San Cristobal, Guadalcanal and Malaita. The protectorate was enlarged to include Rennell and Sikaiana in 1897 and the Eastern Outer Islands in 1898. By the Samoan Tripartite Convention of 1899, Santa Isabel, Choiseul, the Shortlands and Ontong Java were transferred by the Germans in return for the relinquishing of British claims in Samoa.

In 1893, when the protectorate was first proclaimed, there were about fifty Europeans in the Solomons. Five or six were Anglican missionaries and the rest were traders, some of whom owned their own plantations. There was regular schooner communication with Australia. The traders were the usual mixed bunch. In the west Norman Wheatley, who was to be the founder of a well-known island family, arrived at Roviana in 1888 as store manager for two other traders. The local people liked Wheatley and gave him a wife. Two other traders were less popular. In 1890 Peter Pratt Edmunds, otherwise known as French Peter, and Charles Horsman were taken from the Solomons to the High Commissioner's court in Fiji and charged with violent behaviour but were acquitted for want of proper evidence. The only large firm to obtain land in the Solomons before the arrival of the Pacific Islands Company in 1898 and Lever Brothers in the first decade of the twentieth century had been the German company known under the initials DHPG. The German firm made little of its holdings and later sold them.

One of the best-known Europeans in the Solomons in the closing years of the nineteenth century was the naturalist, C. M. Woodford, a large, black-bearded man who travelled extensively in the islands and learned several of the local languages. Between 1885 and 1886 Woodford, based on Bara Island off Guadalcanal, made three unsuccessful attempts to reach the centre of Guadalcanal to collect specimens for the British Museum. Ten years later, in 1896, he was appointed the first Resident Com-

G

missioner of the Solomons, subordinate to the Western Pacific High Commissioner in Fiji. His main duties were to maintain law and order and to attempt to put down head-hunting which was still rampant in the New Georgia area. Tulagi, an island off Guadalcanal, was established as the seat of government and Woodford arrived there from Fiji in 1897 to build a residency. He was accompanied by six policemen, trained in Fiji, and a whaleboat. His instructions were that the protectorate was supposed to be self-supporting.

It was a fantastic job for one man to attempt to control such a wide and lawless area. Just before Woodford's arrival an Austrian geological expedition had been attacked on Mount Tatuve and the following year, 1897, saw the new Resident Commissioner undertaking a punitive expedition on the north coast of Guadalcanal after a newly arrived planter had been killed in a land dispute. In an effort to bring the districts under control, the Resident Commissioner opened a district office at Gizo in the west in 1899, with a Captain Middenway as district officer. Malaita still caused more trouble than the other districts but it was not until 1909 that Woodford was able to establish a district station at Auki on that island.

BACKGROUND OF ISLANDERS

The recorded history of the Solomon Islands in the nineteenth century is almost exclusively the story of the expatriate visitors to the island. Navigators, sea captains, traders, whalers, merchants and missionaries have all left accounts of their time there. But most of these stories are concerned entirely with the white men involved and their immediate circle. The Solomons and the islanders exist mainly as a dark threatening background, occasionally intruding ominously but usually relegated by the white men to comparative obscurity. Some of the missionaries and the odd naturalist or geologist of the stamp of Guppy and Woodford did take an interest in the islanders, and it is from their accounts

106

that we must learn what we can about the reaction of the Solomons to western civilisation and culture, if the way of life offered by the newcomers can be so termed.

For much of the time, of course, island life went on as it had always done. With only fifty expatriates in the group at any one time the white men were bound to have comparatively little influence. Woodford's book *A Naturalist Among the Headhunters*, shows that the islanders' way of life had not changed greatly since the days of Mendana :

> Every morning about eight o'clock, after a light meal of baked yams, men and women start for the gardens in the forest, sometimes as much as three or four miles from the village, a fresh piece of forest being cleared each season. About three in the afternoon, they returned, the women staggering under the weight of huge baskets of yams or sticks of firewood. Flying foxes, birds, prawns or other game they may have killed are not brought home but cooked on a fire on the spot, while the women go home to prepare the evening meal, which is eaten about six o'clock, baked or boiled yams, taro or bananas served in wooden bowls, and a kind of paste scraped off yams, coconuts and other vegetables, boiled in deep wooden bowls, by means of hot stones. Pigs were beaten with clubs and then stifled, then just warmed up on a fire and cut up and distributed.
>
> Each man, no matter how short a distance he may be going, carries a shield of wickerwork, and a tomahawk with a handle about three feet long, some carry spears, but on Guadalcanal bows and arrows are not used for fighting, only small bows and arrows from the midrib of the sago palm for shooting birds or fish. The men often wear a mop-like wig, whitened with lime, and each carries on his shoulder a small bag. The men wear no clothing at all except a T bandage around the waist. On Malaita it is common to see both men and women absolutely naked. I was told sometimes that men had gone to the bush to hunt wild pig, but it was really to kill men, but the men of Guadalcanal were never cannibals as in the other islands. . . .

C. E. Fox, who arrived in the Solomons during the first decade of the twentieth century, has left invaluable accounts of the lives of the people among whom he lived for so many years; and from these we may see that in the eastern district, where he first went, customs and traditions remained unchanged by the arrival of white men in the nineteenth century. Fox does not think that any Solomon Islanders were really cannibals. The Malaita men ate their enemies, but Fox believed that it was merely to emphasise their supremacy over the vanquished, not even to obtain their *mana*. On San Cristobal professional murderers were still in business at the turn of the century, one of them, Sam, having at least sixty-four deaths to his credit or discredit.

Fox also remembers seeing the war canoes of the east going out on expeditions against other islands and sometimes in search of white traders they thought had cheated them. At this time, as for centuries before, the people of San Cristobal were divided into totems, mostly bird totems. Marriages had to be outside the immediate clan, but still within the one-talk system, this being the case on most islands except Malaita. Fighting was rife between villages and between salt-water people and bush people, although on San Cristobal at least the people of the interior spoke the same language and had the same customs as the coastal people.

Many of the customs on San Cristobal were very cruel; on the birth of a first baby the father took it and buried it alive in a hole on the beach; captives brought into a village were either trampled or burned to death. Ancestor worship was practised everywhere. As soon as a man died a relative would come to the door of the house and begin fishing for his soul with a rod and line which he dangled around the corpse until the soul went into a betel nut at the end of the line. The nut was then kept by the family of the dead man. Relatives also fished for the evil spirits which were supposed to live off the flesh of corpses; as soon as the fishing rods began to bend it meant that some of the evil spirits had been caught and could be thrown into the sea.

Various forms of burial were followed on San Cristobal according to age-old custom. If a man was killed in war he was cremated

108

at night. Chieftains, on the other hand, were buried in truncated pyramids up to 30ft high. Each pyramid was built of stone steps rising to a flat platform where sacrifices were offered for the dead. The body of the chief would be laid inside the pyramid but would be taken out every day and carried to a stream by a man of the village whose traditional task it was to wash the corpse in the stream and then carry it back to its resting place. Finally, when only the skeleton remained, it was placed in a canoe and laid on top of the pyramid. That was known as the sky canoe and it was supposed to take the chief up to the sun.

Ordinary men and women were often buried at sea. Spirits of the dead were supposed to make their way to the western end of the island of San Cristobal where there was a rock known as the leaping rock. Here they leapt off the rock into the sea and swam to Paradise which was believed to be located at Rodomana off the Marau Sound near Guadalcanal. There they lived in great happiness, bathing in a river called the water of life and finally becoming united to a supreme being, Aguna, without losing their own personalities.

All over the Solomons such beliefs and customs continued unchanged into the twentieth century : feasts continued to be held, marriages arranged, wars and feuds pursued during the intervals of hunting, gardening, fishing and storytelling. But it would be absurd to pretend that no changes at all had taken place, even if the full effects of them were not yet to be seen. On Malaita and in the other islands labourers were returning from the Queensland sugar plantations. They had seen a new way of life and met people from other islands. Some of them were no longer content to take their ordained place in the clan structure. They began to question the old ways and upset the discipline of the village or district. The traders with their tools and gaudy jewellery and trinkets were persuading men to make copra, and to neglect their gardens in order to do so. The rum offered by these white men drove islanders to wild and foolish deeds. Other islanders, not understanding the white man's laws, thought that when they sold their land to the Europeans it was for just one generation; their children were to discover that the white man regarded the land as theirs for ever.

The missionaries were having their effect as well, sometimes good, sometimes bad. They were bringing Christian education and improved health to the islands, but they were also in some cases condemning the old ways of life. Islanders who became Christians began to be ashamed of their culture and to reject it. The seeds planted in the nineteenth century ripened in the twentieth.

5   PEACE AND WAR

IN spite of a chronic lack of official funds Woodford did an impressive job as the first Resident Commissioner of the Solomons. Having been a frequent visitor to the islands before his appointment he knew both the people and their customs. As Commissioner he was able to keep on good terms with the islanders and the expatriates. His task was far from easy. In his first decade of office a number of epidemics, probably introduced from overseas, swept the islands, killing thousands. Most of the plantation owners seem to have been reasonable men, paying their labourers as much as they could afford, which was not much when the price of copra on the world market was sometimes as little as £4 a ton. One or two of the expatriate plantation owners were less scrupulous in their trading transactions and in their relationships with the local people. This led to a great deal of trouble in the western district at one time. In 1905 the international firm of Lever Brothers entered the Solomons and two years later held 30,000 acres of land under occupancy licence. The managers imported by Levers to look after their holdings were not always of the highest calibre; one of them, P. C. Munster, was deported in 1909 for excessive violence.

It was at this time that Levers made application to import indentured labour from India to work on their plantations. Woodford, who considered the Melanesians to be a dying race, backed this application but the India Office refused to sanction it. Bearing in mind the disturbance caused in Fiji by the importation of Indian workers who today outnumber the native Fijians, it seems to have been a singularly fortunate escape for the Solomon Islanders. Some decades later the Solomons were also considered as a possible site for the major British naval base in the Far East, but the choice fell upon Singapore instead.

In 1910 another trading venture came to the Solomons when the shipping line Burns Philp opened trading stations on Tulagi and in the west and also began buying small plantations. Their ships had been operating in the Solomons area since 1896, and were to continue to do so until 1970. In the same year that Burns Philp opened their trading stations the first Chinese came to the protectorate to work as boat-builders and carpenters for the firm.

After relying for a time on Fijian policemen Woodford did his best to recruit a local force but found it difficult to recruit suitable men. Later time-expired prisoners sometimes had to be relied upon and these were often no more than thugs in uniform. As late as 1916, Sir Hubert Murray, the Lieutenant-Governor of New Guinea, wrote in a letter after visiting the Solomons: 'It is the queerest place imaginable . . . no attempt is made to preserve order or punish crime'. Murray reported that Malaita in particular, and Santa Cruz and Choiseul were not under control. He had visions of New Guinea, German-owned Papua and the Solomons being combined under his governorship, but the idea came to nothing. As an alternative he advocated that the United States should take over all the Pacific islands as they were making such an excellent job of looking after the Philippines.

Meanwhile Woodford did what he could with his small force of policemen and his whale-boat. Occasionally he recruited Europeans as temporary policemen but for major assistance he had to rely on ships sent by the Royal Navy. In 1910 three missionaries were murdered on Rennell and the Resident Commissioner could do little except close the island to outsiders, and when a murder was committed on Malaita Woodford had to appeal for outside asistance, HMS *Torch* being sent to make a punitive raid on the area.

Traditional warfare continued through most of Woodford's tenure of office. As far as can be ascertained the main historical enmities were fairly well defined. In the west the warriors of Mono had captured Fauro and neighbouring small islands, driving out or slaughtering most of the original inhabitants. The head-hunters of Roviana and Simbo were making regular raids on Choiseul and Santa Isabel. The people of the latter island had fled to the south-east corner and were in turn occupying Sandfly. On Malaita the bush people and the salt-water dwellers continued their traditional conflict, taking occasional time off to engage in inter-clan feuds. There were also raids from Malaita on Guadalcanal, the Ariari, a Malaita people, establishing a colony near the Marau Sound. Reciprocal raids from Guadalcanal also took place. The men of Santa Ana hired themselves out as warriors to anyone interested, attacking the coast of San Cristobal frequently. The men of Small Malaita dominated Ulawa and Arosi, while Savo warriors ranged far afield but concentrated particularly on the Russells. Santa Cruz was mainly concerned with rivalry between bush people and salt-water dwellers. In addition to all these activities, of course, there were the local blood feuds in each area.

Official reports of the period emphasise the lawlessness in the protectorate. The Foreign Office report for 1915 admits that 'some years must elapse before complete control of the natives can be brought about', while in 1920 things are no better:

> The natives are restless and warlike, addicted to head-hunting and cannibalism; and on many of the larger islands, especially Malaita and Choiseul, there is incessant warfare. Towards whites they have the reputation of being cruel, treacherous and revengeful.

The 1920 report goes on to suggest that because of the fertility of the soil and the fact that hurricanes and droughts are virtually unknown the Solomons might in time become the largest copra-producing area in the western part of the South Pacific. The supply of labour, however, would have to be increased :

> The natives work on the plantations on the indenture system. The term of employment is for two years for males over sixteen years of age, the main wage being £6 a year for unskilled, £12 for more experienced, and £24 to £36 for really skilled men, housing, food and clothes being supplied. The supply of labour is hopelessly inadequate.

Disease was certainly taking its toll of islanders. Visiting the Solomons in 1921, Dr S. M. Lambert reported :

> Graciosa Bay was so wild that Mr Mathews, Lever Brothers representative, who had lived there fifteen years with an armed guard, warned us not to come ashore. With knives and fish hooks we lured a few of the untamed to come aboard the launch and be examined. In 15 years the population has dropped from 3,000 to 500. Somehow, in spite of their savagery, they had allowed vicious malaria and tuberculosis to get in.

A similar point was made by Hogbin when he visited Ontong Java. The population there had fallen since 1907 from 5,000 to 750. Malaria, tuberculosis, influenza and other diseases were responsible. Hogbin also pointed out that white visitors had tried to root out the old customs and that as a result the old colour and ritual had gone, to be replaced by a monotony of life and a more or less sordid outlook. Collinson, a trader in the area, had less to say about indigenous customs, one of his main complaints being that the government had introduced a law forbidding white men to swear at islanders, the penalty for so doing being a fine of £5.

MORE MISSIONS

For years the Melanesian Mission had had the Solomons to itself, but by the close of the nineteenth century and during the opening decades of the twentieth other denominations began to arrive, as we have already noted (see p 101). In 1898, Bishop Vidal purchased Rua Sura for the Marists, paying £100 to Captain Keating who had previously owned this small island plantation off the north-east coast of Guadalcanal. A year later further Catholic mission stations were opened in the west and on Guadalcanal. The Methodist Mission came in 1902 when the Reverend Dr George Brown arrived at Roviana in the west together with the Reverend J. F. Goldie, two other Europeans, four Fijians, two Samoans, a New Hebridian and one Solomon Islander who had been converted to Christianity while in Fiji, presumably as an indentured labourer. Other islanders had become Methodists while working in the Fijian sugar plantations and a number of them after they had returned to the islands had written to the headquarters of the Wesleyan Methodists, asking for missionaries to be sent to the Solomons. At first the church authorities had hesitated; they had an agreement that they would not encroach on fields being evangelised by the Anglicans, but when on a preliminary visit Brown saw that the Melanesian Mission had not extended as far as the western Solomons he recommended that missionaries be sent there.

The Roviana area was chosen because the Methodists reckoned that if they could convert the fierce Roviana warriors the neighbouring territories would soon follow suit. Brown, who had helped to establish Methodism in New Guinea and was perhaps the best known of all the Wesleyans in the Pacific, came only to establish the Roviana mission. It was then entrusted to Goldie, a hard-working practical man, who had had some financial success in land-dealings in Australasia. Because he had money of his own Goldie impressed the islanders, who thought him a 'big man', unlike the poverty-stricken missionaries in other areas.

Goldie's intense drive certainly helped the spread of Christianity in the western Solomons, but the real architects of its success were those teachers from the other Pacific islands who had come as missionaries with Goldie. These men settled down with the islanders, sharing their food and their way of life; their Christianity was an everyday affair and the islanders could see that it was not forced or put on for their benefit. Not only did

115

these island missionaries bring Christianity to the western Solomons but they brought much else besides. From the Samoans the Solomon Islanders learned methods of weaving; the Tongans showed them how to build their superior outrigger canoes and helped to improve agricultural methods; the Fijians introduced their songs and dances. Methodism soon became widespread in the western islands; and the work of Goldie and his native ministers ensured its supremacy in the area.

Two years after the introduction of Methodism, the South Sea Evangelical Mission came to the Solomons. It was known at that time as the Queensland Kanaka Mission, and had developed in the Queensland sugar fields where it attempted to bring Christianity to the island labourers, of whom there were 13,000 at one period. The director of the mission was Florence Young, who had served as a missionary in China, and its policy was to convert the islanders and then put them in touch with the Christian church in their own areas when they returned home. The Solomons presented a grave problem to the officials of the Queensland Kanaka Mission. They did not want their converts to embrace Catholicism; they suspected the Melanesian Mission of being High Church; and the Methodists were not suitably established in the early years of the century. Then in 1904 labour recruiting for Queensland was forbidden by law, and this meant that thousands of converts would be returning to the Solomons. Miss Young decided that her mission must establish a suitable church for them in the islands.

In fact one convert had already returned to Malaita and had set up his own church. His name was Peter Ambuofa and he had established his mission in his home district on Malaita. Ambuofa was not an educated man and his teaching was extremely muddled, but he was aware of this and sent messages to the mission headquarters in Australia, begging them to send out properly qualified missionaries. One missionary, C. Pullets, had visited Malaita in 1900 but had died after five months there. Others were needed urgently. The first volunteers arrived in 1904.

Three years later, by which time the missionaries were beginning to make progress, the name of the mission was changed to the South Sea Evangelical Mission. An attempt was made to open a mission on the island of Rennell but in 1910 three SSEM missionaries, Thomas Sandwich of the New Hebrides, Tommy Makira of San Cristobal, and Andrew Kanirara, were murdered there. The mission was abandoned and the island closed to Europeans until 1934.

In 1914 another major mission arrived in the Solomons when Norman Wheatley, an old-established European trader, invited Pastor Jones of the Seventh Day Adventist Mission to Gizo in the western islands. Jones inspected Dovele on Vella Lavelle, and then Batuna in the Marovo Lagoon where he set up a station which was headquarters for the mission up to the time of World War II.

BETWEEN THE WARS

Throughout the period of World War I and up to the outbreak of World War II, the Solomons could definitely be regarded as a backwater of the British Empire, ignoring and largely ignored by the outside world. Meanwhile the government of the protectorate concentrated on trying to collect taxes and maintain law and order. Woodford and a handful of district officers did succeed in reducing the incidence of head-hunting and inter-tribal warfare. But with the outbreak of the World War in 1914, government activity was severely restricted and fresh outbreaks of lawlessness ensued, especially on Malaita.

Money was always a problem. The protectorate had to pay its own way out of its revenue, which meant that social services had to be neglected. All education was in the hands of the churches, as were most hospitals, with the exception of the government hospital opened at Tulagi in 1910. It is small wonder that the outside world heard little of the backward and neglected islands of Melanesia. In fact, prior to World War I the only Solomon Islander to achieve anything but local fame was Alec Wickham,

117

the half-breed son of a European planter in the Roviana area of the Solomons. Wickham, an excellent swimmer and diver, was educated in Australia where for some time he toured the country giving exhibitions of spectacular diving and swimming at local carnivals. In 1910 at Sydney he set a world record for the 50yd sprint, and in 1918 claimed a world record for the high dive at Melbourne, plunging, so his manager asserted, 205ft 9in from the cliffs into the river Yarra. Actually the height was about 96ft. Wickham is credited with introducing the first form of the celebrated Australian crawl, this being a variation of the style used for centuries by swimmers of the western Solomons. Wherever he gave his diving exhibition he was billed, to his considerable annoyance, as 'Prince Wickyyama from the Solomons'.

The outbreak of the war in 1914 made little difference to the Solomons: shipping to the islands dropped off and there was some shortage of supplies, but the price of copra rose and plantation owners had some fairly good years. In 1915 Woodford retired and in 1918 C. Workman was appointed Resident Commissioner in his place. By this time it was clear to the islanders that European rule had come to stay. On the whole such supervision was not welcomed. It seemed to the islanders that the government did little for them but impose taxes and put them in prison. Missionaries had condemned their age-old customs and traders cheated them. Diseases introduced by the visitors were sweeping the islands. In 1916 a third of the population of San Cristobal was reported to have died in the previous two or three years from dysentry and chest diseases; in 1920 it was reported that there were three deaths for every birth on San Cristobal.

District officers and resident commissioners came and went, meaning little to most islanders, who seldom saw a white man for more than an hour or so—perhaps when one passed through the village or came ashore for a while from a government vessel. Occasionally there were flashes of 'magic bilong whiteman': in 1926 the first aeroplane was seen in the Solomons when an air-

118

force DH 50A seaplane under the command of Group Captain Williams landed at Kieta, Faisi, Gizo, Batuna and Tulagi on its way from Melbourne.

In 1927 the Solomons emerged from obscurity when a police patrol was massacred on Malaita, two Europeans being among the dead. W. R. Bell, then District Officer on Malaita, was attempting to collect a head tax when the massacre took place. For some time there had been growing discontent on Malaita with the government. As Bell was the only European with whom most of them came into contact they thought that the district officer *was* the government, and that if they killed him there would be no more restrictions. The people particularly objected to the government putting an end to custom fighting and killing, to the outlawing of Snider rifles, and the enclosure of pigs in sties. They could not understand the justice of the authorities who hanged people for justifiable murder when adultery, a much more serious crime in the eyes of a Malaita man, was punished with a small fine or a few weeks in prison.

The massacre did not take place on the spur of the moment. The chief fa'atabu or island priest of the district of Sinerango was much exercised by what he regarded as the injustices imposed by the white administration. He discussed the matter at length with Noru and Mainafoa, the two heads of the other principal clans in his tribe, and they decided to see what the omens had to say about the matter. The fa'atabu, whose name was Basiana, then sacrificed over seventy pigs and decided that the omens were in favour of killing District Officer Bell when he next appeared. The bush people of his district were informed of what the omens had said and how they had been interpreted by their priest. Local informers warned Bell not to go near the Sinerango people, but he ignored their warnings. He told the bush people that he would be at Kwaiambe in the Sinerango sub-district on 4 October and that they were to come down and pay their head-tax of 5s each. The district officer also told the bush people that they were to bring any rifles they owned with them and give them up as

119

their possession was illegal. Bell made this last announcement without obtaining the permission of the Resident Commissioner, Captain R. R. Kane.

On the morning of 4 October some 250 bushmen arrived at Kwaiambe with Basiana, their leader. Bell and a cadet officer named Lillies were already outside the house used as a tax-collecting centre, each sitting at a table, with two policemen and a native clerk in attendance. The rest of the police were inside the leaf house as Bell did not wish unduly to provoke the bush people. At first the islanders formed an orderly queue in order to pay their taxes. Basiana was twenty-first in the line. The bushmen were ordered to put down their firearms before they paid their taxes. Obediently they did so. When it came to his turn Basiana handed over his tax money and walked away. Suddenly he picked up his rifle and ran back towards Bell and Lillies, screaming to the others to join him. Before the district officer could rise, Basiana had smashed the gun down on his head, killing him. The rest of the Sinerango men seized their weapons and attacked the police party, smashing their way into the house. Cadet Lillies, the clerk, twelve policemen and some servants were killed in the onslaught. The rest managed to escape before the bushmen turned and ran back into the interior. Priests from the neighbouring mission of Nivanca looked after the survivors and gave a Christian burial to those who had been killed.

The Sinerango killings caused an uproar which reached the newspapers of the western world. The Resident Commissioner re-acted—some felt over-reacted—quickly. A volunteer force was raised from among European residents and HMS *Adelaide* was dispatched from Sydney. The cruiser shelled all the villages up the coast as far as Ata'a and practically all the male members of the Sinerango tribe were arrested. Police patrols hunted Basiana for months before finally arresting him. A judicial commissioner arrived from Fiji and the ringleaders were brought to trial. Basiana and five others were hanged and eighteen imprisoned. Of 198 people originally arrested, 25 died, mainly from dysentry,

120

Page 121 The younger generation: (above) young women of Kia, Santa Isabel, look on with interest and amusement at a dancing festival; (below) boys of Sasamungga, Choiseul

Page 122 Schools: *(above)* primary school class at Santa Isabel; *(below)* school-children on parade at Santa Cruz, with school itself in middle distance on left

during their period of detention. Most of the men of the tribe were moved to Tulagi for a while, while the women and children were made to go and live at Uru. The authorities considered deporting the whole tribe to another island, but decided against it. Eventually the people were allowed back to their former homes in the mountains.

As a result of the Sinerango murders, the Secretary of State for the Colonies directed that an official inquiry be carried out. This investigation was made by Sir H. C. Moorhouse. His report pointed out, among others things, that headmen had been badly chosen in the past and that much greater care must be taken in their future selection as it was essential that they should be acceptable to their own people. Mention was made of the power wielded in the villages by teachers trained by the SSEM.

After the Moorhouse Report began the slow progress towards the system of native councils and native courts introduced in the 1940s. A number of people felt that it should be speeded up. Between 1929 and 1934 a popular European priest of the Melanesian Mission, Richard Fallowes, urged the men of Santa Isabel, Savo and Nggela to demand representation on the nominated advisory council. Fallowes had a large following and the movement spread to San Cristobal. A flag was prepared and requests for higher wages put to government. The authorities moved in quickly and the priest was asked to leave. With his departure the movement (sometimes known as the 'chair and rule' movement from the chair and wooden rule which were symbols of native administration) languished and came to nothing.

In the 1930s government continued to be administered from Tulagi. J. S. Phillips, visiting the Solomons, wrote this about the situation as he saw it :

> There are about 95,000 natives in the Solomons and perhaps three dozen government officers. Nearly all these latter—say 30 —live with their families on Tulagi, a small islet with a club, golf links, and tennis court, miles away from the wild, jungle-covered islands, where live the bulk of the native population.

H

Phillips went on to say that it was generally considered that the best work of the government was done by the seven or eight district officers and cadets who between them had to administer the great bush and salt-water areas. It was perhaps unfair to criticise the administration too strongly. It was hampered throughout the between-war years by lack of funds and lack of interest on the part of Great Britain. Plantation owners, badly hit by the slump in world copra prices, which had tumbled from £40 to less than £10 a ton, found it difficult to make ends meet. They paid their labourers badly and this caused resentment, particularly at Gizo and on Malaita. Missionaries continued to make themselves largely responsible for health and education as well as for the spiritual welfare of the islanders. Apart from a brief rush of gold-miners to Guadalcanal in the 1930s, little else of moment occurred until 1942.

JAPANI HA-HA!

In 1942 when war came to the Solomons only a few Europeans were living in the islands—a number of government officers, some missionaries, planters, traders and miners. Then the Japanese began their advance across the Pacific and for virtually the first time the Solomons became important to the outside world. After their sudden attack on Pearl Harbour in 1941 the Japanese had driven all before them, capturing island after island in the Pacific. In March 1942, Bougainville was seized. It seemed that the British Solomon Islands Protectorate would be taken with as much ease.

There was only a token force of troops in the Solomons. A few Australian riflemen were charged with the responsibility of guarding a small seaplane base with its solitary Catalina near Tulagi, off the coast of Guadalcanal. The Resident Commissioner, W. S. Marchant, issued orders for the formation of a Solomon Islands Defence Force which in the first instance consisted of three officers, two non-commissioned officers and a hundred and twelve other ranks recruited from government officers and members of the native constabulary. The remaining administrative officers were later given commissioned rank in this force.

It was apparent that the Solomons were going to play a vital part in the Pacific campaign. The islands lay in the path of the Japanese advance on Fiji, Australia and New Zealand. They also were ideally situated for an Allied counter-attack, a fact which was recognised by the American Chiefs of Staff when in March 1942 they informed President Roosevelt that an attack on Japanese-occupied New Guinea would have to be launched from the obscure island of Guadalcanal in the Solomons. In the same month Japanese aircraft had begun regular heavy bombing raids on Tulagi and the adjoining islands.

The Resident Commissioner ordered that all civilians should be evacuated from Tulagi by ship and this was undertaken in conditions of some confusion, the rescue vessel being bombed as it took on its passengers. In some ways it was the end of an era in the Solomons. For the first time islanders saw large numbers of Europeans in a panic; if there had ever been any aura of white supremacy in the Solomons it was dispelled on the day of that chaotic evacuation of Tulagi. Another aspect of the flight noticed by those who remained was that no provision seemed to have been made for the rescue of the Chinese workers, hereditary enemies of the advancing Japanese. Later the Chinese were removed to the safety of another island where most of them sat out the war years although some skilled workers returned to Tulagi when it had been retaken by the marines.

Some civilians remained, among them missionaries, traders and planters and a few miners. They chose not to board the vessel *Morinda* at Tulagi in case they could be of use in the Solomons. Most of them were recruited by the organisation known simply as the coastwatchers, and so were a number of government officers. This body had been organised from Australia by Lieutenant-Commander Eric Feldt of the Royal Australian Navy. The coastwatchers were to be intelligence agents behind

125

the Japanese lines in the islands of the South Pacific. Each man was provided with a heavy radio transmitter and receiver and then allocated a prearranged position from where it would be possible to report on enemy movements.

A nucleus of government officers was sent out to the islands almost at once. On Guadalcanal, Martin Clemens, a young district officer who had hurried back to the Solomons from leave in Australia, was given the district sub-station of Aola on the north coast of the island. Other coastwatchers appointed were Wilson in the east, Forster on San Cristobal, Kennedy in the west and Macfarlane near Lunga on Guadalcanal. Three other Europeans were already installed on Guadalcanal and refused to move; these were K. D. Hay, a planter; A. M. Andresen, a gold miner; and F. A. Rhoades, a former plantation manager.

Marchant, the Resident Commissioner, elected to move his administrative headquarters to Malaita, as it was obvious that the Japanese would soon be arriving at Tulagi. All island labourers who had been working on plantations were returned by small ships to their homes, and the district officers toured their islands talking to the people. The theme of their message was simple : the Japanese would soon be arriving, the islanders were not to help them. The British would be returning.

It was a period of great confusion for the islanders. Most of the white people, including the Australian soldiers and the seaplane crew, had left. The people known as 'Japani' were in Bougainville. The people of the Solomons were being asked to remain loyal to a British rule few of them knew anything about, except in the context of tax-collections and discipline. In the event the islanders were amazingly loyal in a war that can have meant little to them. After the flight of some of the plantation owners there was a little indiscriminate looting, and at one juncture later on some islanders went down to the coast to offer their services as labourers to the Japanese, but a chance air strike from American aeroplanes terrified them and drove them back into the bush. Otherwise the islanders served as guides, labourers and even in some unofficial cases as fighting men for the Allies.

On 3 May 1942, some three weeks after occupying the Short-lands in the west, a Japanese naval force steamed unopposed into the deserted harbour at Tulagi. Ships under Admiral Goto disembarked troops, anti-aircraft guns and radio communications personnel. Twenty-four seaplanes arrived later. By chance, air-craft from an American task force steaming through the area sighted the Japanese unloading at Tulagi on 4 May, and attacked, sinking one destroyer and damaging two minesweepers and a number of berthed seaplanes.

At Aola on Guadalcanal, Martin Clemens waited for the Japanese to cross the strip of water from Tulagi. With him were sixty islanders who had volunteered to join the British Solomon Islands Defence Force. Between them they had twelve rifles, later increased to eighteen, and some ammunition abandoned by the Australian troops before they left. Clemens had also established a system of scouts using canoes and keeping him in touch with what was happening at Tulagi. At the end of May the first Japanese party moved over from Tulagi. Clemens left Aola and moved into the interior, making camp at the village of Vungana. On 1 July, Dovu, one of Clemens's scouts, hurried up the moun-tain path to report to the district officer that the Japanese were landing in force on the north coast of Guadalcanal. For two months the Japanese occupied Guadalcanal unopposed. Their men on the island were mainly construction workers and their main task seemed to be the building of an airfield. Clemens watched and sent regular messages to Australia and New Zealand. Constantly he wondered when the Allies would make some attempt to recapture the island.

The Americans had decided as early as March that Guadal-canal and Tulagi must be retaken so that they could serve as a springboard for an assault on the western Solomons and New Guinea. The man entrusted with the task was General Alexander Archer Vandegrift, commander of the 1st Marine Division.

Vandegrift, a veteran of over thirty years' service, was not informed until 26 June that his attack was to take place at the beginning of August. Startled, he asked for more time. He had been in New Zealand when the news had been sprung on him and his men were scattered, some in Samoa and others somewhere on the high seas between San Francisco and Auckland. He had expected to command the amphibious assault some time in 1943, not at five weeks' notice. No respite was allowed, but he was given the 2nd Marines of 2nd Division to reinforce his command.

The general did what he could. From Auckland he sent his intelligence officers to Australia to seek out anyone with practical knowledge of the Solomons. Eight veterans of the islands volunteered or were persuaded to accompany the assault force and act as guides. Working against time Vandegrift tried desperately to prepare for the landing, collating intelligence reports, working out his plan of battle and organising the loading and unloading of supplies.

At one point the weather in New Zealand was so bad that the dockers refused to work, so Vandegrift cleared them out of the docks and his own marines acted as labourers, working in eight-hour shifts round the clock. He again begged to be allowed to postpone the date of the attack; he was given one extra week and told that Guadalcanal and Tulagi must be invaded on 7 August. The commander knew that he would be landing virtually 'blind'. There were no adequate maps of the area to be invaded and events were to show that the estimates of some of the planters and traders consulted were widely at variance with the facts. Matters were not helped when specially commissioned aerial photographs were lost before they could be properly studied.

In the end Vandegrift and his staff produced a plan of attack. There were to be two assaults, one on Guadalcanal and the other on Tulagi and the adjacent islands of Gavatu, Tanambogo and the Florida group. The best-trained force, consisting of 1st Raider

Battalion, 1st Parachute Battalion and 2nd Battalion 5th Marines under the overall command of Brigadier-General William H. Rupertus, were to attack Tulagi where the enemy would be unable to retreat and would have to stand and fight. On Guadalcanal, on the other hand, it was assumed that the Japanese might elect to retreat into the interior. For the assault on that island Vandegrift selected the remainder of 1st Marine Division under his own leadership.

In all, 959 officers and 18,156 men embarked in a naval force consisting of the US aircraft carriers *Saratoga*, *Enterprise* and *Wasp*, the battleship *North Carolina* and an escort of cruisers and destroyers. A rehearsal of the projected landing was carried out at Fiji. It was a fiasco. Greatly depressed, Vandegrift gave the order for the expeditionary force to proceed to the Solomons for the real attack.

Because of a shortage of landing craft it was not possible to launch the two attacks simultaneously. At Tulagi the Raiders under Edson were to go ashore on the south side, followed by 2nd Battalion 5th Marines. Both units were then to fight their way inland and advance to the east. The Parachute Battalion was to go ashore at the twin islands of Gavatu and Tanambogo. On Guadalcanal the landing was to be effected east of the Lunga area. The Americans anticipated that there would be about 5,000 Japanese on the island, a gross over-estimate. The bulk of 5th Marines would go ashore first and establish a beachhead, and would be followed by 1st Marines. An attack to the west of the island would follow.

On 7 August the Americans attacked the Solomon Islands. At dawn aircraft from their carriers bombed Tulagi, Gavatua and Tanambogo, while their ships bombarded both Guadalcanal and Tulagi. American forces then went ashore at Tulagi. With them went two former administrative officers from the Solomons, D. C. Horton and A. N. Waddell, both of whom were awarded the Silver Star for their part in the fighting that day. The Japanese on Tulagi fought desperately but were overwhelmed after two days of hard combat, and Tulagi and the adjacent islands were all taken by the Americans.

The landing at Guadalcanal was unopposed. The marines went ashore east of Lunga Point, between the Tenaru river and Tenevatu Creek. Troops of the 5th and 1st US Marines landed, supported by fire from three cruisers and four destroyers, and by 75mm howitzers from 11th Marines, which came ashore with the assault battalions. Later in the day, 105mm howitzers from the 11th Marines were landed. The 1st Battalion of 5th Marines advanced west along the beach towards the Lunga river, while 1st Marines advanced against sporadic fire south-west towards Mount Austen. The 3rd Battalion of 5th Marines, with artillery, engineer, pioneer, and special weapons and defence battalions were scheduled to hold the beach during the advance.

Apart from a few hasty shots from the retreating Japanese, the landing had been relatively easy. But while the troops got ashore without trouble, the supplies did not. There had been insufficient planning and huge piles of stores mounted on the beach with no one to move then inland; at one time landing craft were hovering off the coast trying to find a place to come ashore, dump their stores and go back to the fleet for more. The other major drawback was the lack of accurate maps. Vandegrift had been informed that Mount Austen was close to the beach and could be reached the first day. In fact it was some miles inland and beyond the reach of heavily laden and inexperienced troops, so the order to proceed to Mount Austen had to be countermanded.

At dusk on 7 August, 1st Battalion of 5th Marines established a perimeter defence at the mouth of the Ilu river, while the three battalions of 1st Marines dug in for the night in the jungle—as the Americans at first termed Lever's Lunga Plantation—about 3,500yd to the south. By 8pm on 7 August, 10,000 American troops had come ashore. The first night was a noisy one. Unused to the sounds of the bush, troops constantly fired at what they thought were enemy troops. The Japanese, however, had fled earlier that day.

On 8 August, 1st Battalion of 5th Marines crossed the Ilu and Lunga rivers and seized Kukum village, making their first contact with Japanese troops, who were overrun on the outskirts of Kukum. Meanwhile, troops, supplies and equipment continued to land on the beaches near Lunga Point, harassed by raids from Japanese bombers.

The primary objective of the American landing force was the capture of the airfield under construction by the Japanese at Lunga. From information given to the United States Intelligence by coastwatchers at Gold Ridge, overlooking the airfield, it was estimated that there were about 500 Japanese and approximately 2,500 Korean labourers in the airfield area. The airfield was occupied by the Americans on 9 August, almost without opposition as the Japanese and Koreans had now retired either to the hills or along the course of the Matanikau river. The 1st Engineer Battalion began work on the uncompleted surface of the airstrip.

The same evening American and Australian naval forces between Guadalcanal and Savo suffered a crushing defeat at the hands of Japanese ships which had crept unobserved from New Guinea down to the Solomons. One coastwatcher sent warning of the approach of the ships, but the British Royal Naval commander of the Allied force was away from his vessels at a meeting with General Vandegrift and Admiral Ghormley at the time and left no plan of battle action with his officers. In a night attack lasting only thirty minutes and known afterwards as the Battle of Savo, Japanese ships sank the American cruisers *Astoria*, *Vincennes* and *Quincy*, and HMAS *Canberra*. Had the Japanese admiral gone a little farther he would have sunk the Americans transports lying defenceless off the shore, but his flagship had been damaged and he feared an American air strike. On his way back to New Guinea one of the Japanese ships was sunk but there could be no doubt that the Americans and Australians had suffered a considerable blow.

To make matters worse, the American naval commander decided that he could not hazard his remaining vessels by leaving them in Solomon waters. He at once withdrew his three aircraft carriers and other vessels, leaving the marines on Guadalcanal with no naval support and with only half their supplies unloaded. Doggedly Vandegrift gave the order to his marines to dig in on Guadalcanal. A perimeter defence along 9,600yd of shore line from the mouth of the Ilu river to the village of Kukum was the area chosen to be defended.

The most important part of the area was the airstrip, named Henderson Field after Major Lofton Henderson, a marine hero of the Battle of Midway Island. On 10 August, the day after the airstrip had been taken, General Vandegrift announced that it would be capable of being used by thirty-six fighters and nine scout bombers; it was reported ready for operation on 17 August. American aircraft began to arrive; possession of the airstrip proving the trump card in the Americans' hands. For some time, however, the field was badly short of essential equipment and men—ground crews, bomb hoists and repair facilities.

The Japanese determined that Henderson Field must be their main objective if they were to recapture Guadalcanal. All their efforts were bent to this. On 18 August they began landing reinforcements at Taivu Point and at Kakambona. For months the Japanese had naval supremacy and their regular convoys of men and supplies from New Guinea and the western Solomons became known as the 'Tokyo Express'. Before the end of the campaign they had 30,000 troops on Guadalcanal. Eventually the Americans and their allies outnumbered the enemy, with a total in excess of 50,000, but at first the Japanese, with their command of the sea, had the advantage.

The first large-scale attack took place at the mouth of the Ilu river. The maps owned by the Americans were so faulty that they thought the river was the Tenaru. A determined Japanese drive across the river was repulsed after a bloody bout of hand-to-hand fighting and when the Japanese finally withdrew they left 800 dead.

Shortages of men and weapons imposed severe limitations on

the marine garrison at Lunga Point, and until more troops arrived it was impossible to take offensive action to keep the Japanese beyond artillery range of Henderson Field. Meanwhile the 'Tokyo Express' was bringing more Japanese troops to the island. The defenders of the airfield were heavily bombed and shelled; supplies began to run short; the rain seemed incessant; their vehicles churned up vast amounts of mud, and in addition to all the attendant discomforts of the hot and humid climate large numbers of Americans were affected by malaria.

On 13 and 14 September the Japanese made a major thrust at Henderson Field; it was known afterwards as the Battle of Bloody Ridge. Wave after wave of Japanese soldiers were driven off by the Americans from their dug-outs. Colonel Merritt Edson's 1st Raider Battalion defended the low grassy ridge at the edge of the airstrip with great courage. Edson himself received the Medal of Honour for his leadership.

A month later the Japanese again attacked in the direction of Henderson Field. General Hyakutake's soldiers carved a road through the jungle from Kakambona to a position south of the airstrip. The trail was fifteen miles long. Working in incredibly difficult conditions the army engineers had the track completed by 16 October. On that date the Japanese started to march towards Henderson Field. Existing on half-rations of rice, moving through a constant torrential downpour, each man carrying one artillery shell in addition to his normal equipment, thousands of them struggled through the jungle, moving at a rate of six miles a day for five days. An entire army was in position by 22 October, but it was an army without heavy artillery for the field pieces had been abandoned on the way.

On 23 October, after a light artillery barrage, the Japanese attacked again and only a short distance from Bloody Ridge, the scene of their original defeat. Unfortunately for the Japanese General Sumiyoshi, in charge of one section of the total onslaught, had not been informed that the attack was postponed by one day. Accordingly he took his men across the Matanikau and with nothing else to distract them the Americans were able to deal effectively with Sumiyoshi's force. Six hundred and fifty soldiers were killed before the remainder withdrew.

The next day the main Japanese force attacked east of the Lunga river. Marines and men of the 16th US Infantry Regiment held their ground. The fury of the Japanese attack exceeded anything that had gone before. The Americans wavered and it looked as if they would break. An elated Japanese general sent back to his headquarters the code-word *Banzai*, indicating that Henderson Field had fallen. The signal was premature. The Japanese Sendai Division reached the perimeter of the field but the Americans rallied and drove it back. Most of the combat was at close quarters. General Geiger, in command of the US forces, sent in his last reinforcements. They were enough to decide the issue. At dawn the Japanese withdrew, leaving 900 dead on the slopes of the ridge.

Then Japanese naval vessels off the coast began pounding shells into the American lines. Aircraft of the so-called Catcus Airforce, piloted by men like Joe Foss, supreme American air-ace, staggered into the air. Japanese Zero aircraft coming in to bomb the American lines were driven away. The Japanese destroyers were less easy to dispose of. Altogether it was a bad day for the Americans trying to repair their lines. Seven air attacks, the shelling from the sea and the attentions of the Japanese artillery piece known as 'Pistol Pete' caused that day to be known as 'Dugout Sunday'.

At dusk the Japanese troops attacked again. As many as 200 men at a time hurled themselves at American defensive positions. Again the issue hung in the balance. At one sector the Japanese broke through but were forced back by a hastily recruited band of clerks, messengers and bandsmen. At close range the American's mortars and rifles began to mow down the Japanese. Long-range artillery fire completed the carnage. By dawn it was all over; the Japanese had gone. They did not return.

By 29 October the Japanese were retreating eastward and westward. They had lost more than 2,000 men in less than a week. Two weeks later a large convoy of Japanese troop transports were bombed by American aircraft and then attacked by US warships. Ten transports were destroyed and only 4,000 of an estimated 10,000 Japanese troops got ashore at Guadalcanal. This was the last major effort by the Japanese army and navy to recapture the Lunga area by a co-ordinated attack. Thereafter, the most important factor of the Guadalcanal campaign was the long, hard ground fighting on the island itself. Some further Japanese reinforcements were brought in, and from Kakambona to Lunga along the coast and in the hills, United States marines, army troops, planes and artillery continued bitter fighting against the desperately brave Japanese.

One of the most difficult of the minor skirmishes of the Guadal-canal campaign was that in which Lieutenant-Colonel Evans F. Carlson's 2nd Raider Battalion was involved. After a sizeable Japanese force had broken through the American lines and headed for the safety of the interior, Carlson's Raiders took to the bush after the Japanese. Between 11 and 18 November they fought a series of running battles with the Japanese, and then pursued them into the mountains, living off the land and attacking the Japanese whenever they caught up with them. Before returning to base the Raiders lived in the interior for thirty days. They had fought twelve minor battles and killed over four hundred of the Japanese.

Finally, after a very closely contested campaign, the Americans got the upper hand on Guadalcanal. Their success was due to a number of factors: the steadfastness and courage of the American troops and their officers; the establishment of air supremacy at Henderson Field; the arrival of supporting Australian, Fijian and New Zealand troops and the work of the coastwatchers—indeed Admiral Halsey later declared that the coastwatchers had saved Guadalcanal and that Guadalcanal saved the Pacific.

This seems now to be an accepted fact. The Guadalcanal campaign is recognised as the turning point of the war in the

Pacific. Before Guadalcanal the Japanese had been advancing. After it they were always retreating. One Japanese general claimed that the island was the graveyard of the Japanese army. No accurate figure has ever been released of the Japanese casualties on the island : it is known that the Americans lost 1,500; Japanese losses have been estimated as being between 20,000 and 30,000. These figures might have been much larger had it not been for the brilliantly executed withdrawal staged by the Japanese army and naval forces when thousands of troops were embarked under cover of darkness in February and transported away from Guadalcanal without the Americans knowing anything about it until it was too late.

After the Guadalcanal campaign was over, fighting in the western Solomons continued. For some time coastwatchers had been active in the area, particularly Douglas Kennedy who, with a small fleet of vessels and the aid of picked islanders had been waging what was practically a private war against the Japanese. It was another coastwatcher in the west, Reg Evans, who arranged the rescue of John F. Kennedy when his PT 109 had been cut in half by a Japanese destroyer; and in many cases coastwatchers played a vital part in the celebrated series of island-hopping raids carried out in 1943 by Americans, Fijians, Tongans and New Zealanders, when the Allies attacked the Japanese at such places as Munda airfield, Vella Lavella and Treasury Island, before proceeding to Bougainville. In the western islands campaign Corporal Sefanaia Sukanaivalu of the Fijian forces was posthumously awarded the Victoria Cross. Badly wounded, Corporal Sukanaivalu was lying in no-man's land between the Japanese and his own platoon. Knowing that members of his platoon were going to risk death by coming out to rescue him, the corporal deliberately raised himself in front of the enemy machine guns and was killed at once.

Most of the fighting in the western Solomons had ended by the closing weeks of 1943, but pockets of the enemy continued to hold out until 1944 and even into the following year. The last

Japanese soldier to give himself up did so in Guadalcanal in 1947 when he was caught stealing food from the gardens of the policemen behind the police barracks in Honiara, the new capital.

With scarcely an exception the islanders remained loyal to the Allies throughout the war. One Santa Isabel man and one western islander are known to have helped the Japanese. For the rest, Solomon Islanders were of the utmost service to the Americans and the coastwatchers. They acted as scouts and guides, rescued soldiers cut off from their units and helped crashed flyers. As labourers and bearers they were always in evidence. It has been suggested that more islanders would have helped the Japanese if the latter had treated them better. It is true that after an initial attempt to be friendly the Japanese did nothing to endear themselves to the islanders : they looted gardens, pressed islanders into service without pay and in some areas towards the end of the campaign when they were retreating, shot any islander they came across.

Individual Solomon Islanders became famous for their martial exploits. Chief among them was Sergeant-major Jacob Vouza, a former member of the Solomon Islands Armed Constabulary. Vouza had retired on a pension in 1940 and later became the subject of a book, Hector Macquarrie's *Vouza and the Solomon Islands*. When the Japanese invaded the Solomons, Vouza volunteered to serve in the BSIP Defence Force and was enlisted as a scout. After leading a number of raiding and search parties he was eventually captured by the Japanese and tied to a tree. He refused to betray the whereabouts of American troops in the area although tortured by his captors. He was bayoneted in the neck and body and left for dead. He escaped and crawled back to the American lines, where he made a full report before allowing himself to be taken to hospital. Later he wrote down his account of what had happened to him.

> Well, I was caughted by the Japs and one of the Japanese officers questioned me but I was refuse to answer and I was bayoneted by a long sword twice on my chest, through my

137

throat, and cutted the side of my tongue and I was got up
from the enemies and walked through the American front line.

Vouza was awarded both the British George Medal and the
American Silver Star for his wartime exploits. In 1957 he was
made a Member of the Order of the British Empire, having
served as headman, president of the Guadalcanal Council and
the BSIP Advisory Council. He also received from a visiting
American television personality a cherished gift of a set of false
teeth. Vouza was also involved in the post-war Marching Rule
movement, but not, it would appear, too enthusiastically.

Another Solomon Islander who attained distinction during the
war was Bill Bennett, the son of a New Zealand father and a
Solomon Island mother. Today Bennett is in charge of the local
broadcasting service, the first Solomon Islander to become head
of a government department. During the war he acted as chief
scout to coastwatcher D. C. Kennedy in the western Solomons.
Kennedy's headquarters in the west served as a rallying point for
many islanders who wished to help the Allies and the two of them
were involved in a number of hand-to-hand battles with the
Japanese. Once the schooner on which Bennett was moored was
set on fire and sunk by the Japanese but Bennett and his crew
dived over the side and swam to safety. On another occasion
Kennedy and Bennett in a 10-ton schooner rammed and sank a
Japanese whale-boat, both being wounded in the encounter. At
one time the New Zealander and the Solomon Islander, miles
behind the Japanese lines, had their own stockade in which they
kept their prisoners of war. Bennett was awarded the Military
Medal for charging a beached Japanese barge when armed only
with a tommy-gun.

Ben Kevu from Wana Wana Island was the scout who rescued
John F. Kennedy. He and seven other islanders paddled in canoes
to a small island near Gizo where there had been reports of eleven
stranded American sailors. Kevu found them and took their
officer Lieutenant Kennedy back to Gomu Island where coastwatcher A. R. Evans was waiting. The coastwatcher arranged

Page 139 (above) School children in typical canoe off Duff Islands—most children own their own canoes; *(below)* young villagers of Manawai, Malaita

Page 140 (above) Gossiping at Haemarao, south coast of Guadalcanal; (below)
Sasamungga market, Choiseul. The people come to buy and sell fruit and vegetables
and meet friends

for Kennedy and his men to be transported back to their base. After the war Kevu was taken to the United States where he appeared on television and met again the man he had rescued.

Seni, from the western district, started the war with one rifle, but by stalking any Japanese foolish enough to come his way he soon possessed thirty-two and armed his own force with them. Another man, Ngatu, led a party of men into a Japanese camp while the Japanese slept and stole all their weapons. When the Japanese awoke they found themselves surrounded, with one rifle in their possession. These and many other islanders fought fiercely against the Japanese, especially during their retreat, when many groups of the enemy were cut off in the jungle and slaughtered by the islanders.

The last Japanese detachment surrendered on Choiseul in 1945 and it was two or three years more before the last Americans left the Solomons. In these few years there had been many and unsettling changes. Off the shores were hulls of wrecked ships; crashed aeroplanes were everywhere; practically every village had an empty shell casing as a church bell. The islanders had seen slaughter on a scale they had never dreamt of. The Americans and their Allies had not only brought thousands of vehicles and machines to the islands but also their film shows and entertainments and the whole impact of a completely different way of life.

MARCHING RULE

BEFORE the end of World War II there were already stir-
rings in the Solomons of the quasi-national movement
which was to become known as Marching Rule. This
movement had its roots in a number of causes and is believed to
have started in 1943 or 1944. There had been some unrest on
plantations before the war, as early as 1935 on Malaita, and also
in the west. Discipline was imposed harshly by a number of expatriate overseers and managers, whips and dogs being used by
some. In 1939 islanders were already refusing to work on the
more notorious plantations.

It was after the fighting was over on Guadalcanal, however,
that the Marching Rule movement got under way, while the
large United States occupation force was on the island. Many
Solomon Islanders working in the labour force came into increasing contact with the Americans and found them much more
friendly than the British administrators and Australian plantation
managers, both of whom, the islanders thought, treated the natives
as 'rubbish men'. They saw that the coloured American soldiers
were wearing the same clothes as the white Americans, eating the
same food and using the same equipment. All Americans were extremely generous, paying well for services and giving away equipment apparently regardless of cost. This generosity prevented any
American being regarded as a 'big man' for a big man demands
value for money, but it increased the islanders' liking for their
visitors. When some of the Americans began to decry British

142

colonialism and told the islanders that they should govern their own affairs when the war ended, there were many attentive listeners.

Although the official Volunteer Labour Force received low wages, the Americans paid as much as £14 a month to islanders who worked for them, and were generous with gifts of army-issue fuel and food. This so impressed the islanders, especially the Malaita and Nggela men, that in 1943 some of them attempted to 'buy' American rule. Their money was accepted for the Red Cross and this convinced some of the islanders that they were now under American protection. When the British Resident Commissioner heard of this he insisted that at least part of the money should be paid back.

Many islanders were convinced that the Americans would stay in the Solomons after the war. This seems to have been one of the reasons for the loss of face and prestige suffered by the British and Australians; not because many of them left in 1942 but because administration in the Solomons between 1942 and 1945 appeared to have emanated either from the Japanese or the Americans, the British Resident Commissioner and his staff playing a minor role. In 1944 efforts were made to persuade the islanders that the Americans would eventually leave, the American authorities themselves informing Nori, one of the leaders of the Marching Rule movement, that all United States troops would be going home after the war.

In spite of this assurance, many islanders continued to believe that the Americans would return one day, bringing with them many ships full of food and other goods, a belief that blossomed into the millennial cargo-cult element of the Marching Rule movement. One of the first outward signs of dissension occurred in 1944 when a number of Malaita men returning home after service refused to accept the authority of the government-appointed headman at Ata'a, a village near the Lau Lagoon and in the same general area as Sinerango where Bell and Lillies had been murdered almost twenty years before.

From this small beginning the movement spread rapidly. By 1945 Guadalcanal, north Malaita, Ulawa and San Cristobal had been affected and the Florida group joined in later. Marching Rule never really caught on in the western Solomons, and the islands in this district remained largely outside the events of the next few years, although today there are Solomon Islanders who declare that when eventually detachments of police were sent to Malaita these units consisted largely of recruits from the west, traditional enemies of Malaita people.

One of the impressive facts about the movement was that although it brought Solomon Islanders together, working in amity for the first time in some areas, it allowed a great deal of autonomy in its organisation. One of the dominating personalities of the early days of Marching Rule was Nori, a middle-aged man who had worked on plantations and by island standards was not unfamiliar with expatriates and their way of life. It was said, by his followers, that he had been inspired by the sight of an American general smoking a golden pipe and that this general had told him that if he wished to become rich he would have to start Marching Rule. Another leader, at least in the early stages, was Timothy George, the son of a Solomon Islander who had gone to work in the Australian sugar fields. He was born and educated in Australia where he learnt to speak and write English, and when he returned to the Solomons in 1910 he was made much of by one of the missions as an islander who could also communicate with expatriates. He was not involved in the beginnings of the movement but took advantage of it once it was under way.

One of the first 'big men' in Marching Rule was a Malaita district headman known as Hoasihau, a nephew of a great *ramo* called Arisimae. Hoasihau, sharing the general disaffection, held a series of meetings for the purposes of gathering enough money to hire a chief who would negotiate with the Europeans. At about the same time in the Waisisi area of Malaita, Nori and Aliki Nonohimae started to collect money for much the same end, though they claimed that the money was to buy a plantation and

144

hire European experts. The Ariari and Koio districts became centres of nationalist activity on Malaita, but when a group of families moved from the Lau Lagoon and settled in Walande on Small Malaita they found a similar movement in progress there. Timothy George assumed the leadership on Small Malaita and sent a deputation of 300 men to march up to Ariari and Koio and as far as eastern Kwara'ae, telling people what was happening. Then he and Nori met and assumed joint leadership on Malaita. Today some islanders who were involved claim that Timothy George was allowed to link up with Nori because his knowledge of English would enable him to negotiate with the authorities, but that a number of Marching Rule adherents, even at that time, did not consider the Walande man to be tough enough for the leadership. It is a fact that Timothy George lost enthusiasm for the movement towards the end and that he did not share the eventual imprisonment of the other leaders.

In the initial stages at any rate, Timothy George was both enthusiastic and efficient. He and Nori divided Malaita into nine districts, roughly the same as the government administrative districts, and asked each district to select a 'head chief' to be responsible for Marching Rule in that area. The leaders were soon forthcoming; of the nine elected 'head chiefs', six were mission-educated school teachers. Occasionally all the 'head chiefs' met together but for most of the time each man ran his own district with the assistance of 'full chiefs' who ranked just below the 'head chiefs'. Clerks were employed to help each chief and bands of young men armed with clubs were formed to act as bodyguards. These bodyguards were supervised by 'strife chiefs' who trained them and drilled them so that they could form guards of honour for any visiting chieftains. In the gardens work was supervised by 'farmer chiefs'.

There has been a certain amount of discussion about the origins of the term Marching Rule. When news of the movement first reached Great Britain some newspapers with more ingenuity than accuracy claimed that it was a corruption of

'Marxian Rule' and was a communist-inspired movement. The most generally accepted version is that the name comes from 'Masinga Rule', *masinga* being an Ariari word meaning brother or brotherhood (and also 'young shoot of the taro'), but some people hold that it comes from the South Sea Evangelical Mission song which began 'The SSEM is marching along, marching along. . .'.

The organisation of the movement on Malaita was excellent until internal antagonisms and dissensions began to rend it. Courts were set up, supervised by 'custom chiefs', and these dealt with breaches of customs approved by the movement, refusal to adhere to the principles of the cult or to pay its taxes. The custom chief or *alaha'ohu* became very important and influential as it was he who apprehended offenders, had them brought before his court and if they were found guilty fined them or sentenced them to a term in the Marching Rule prison. The British administration had itself set up native courts between 1942 and 1944, a considerable step, but their powers had been limited. Even so, the Marching Rule courts were not intended to try such serious offences as murder, manslaughter, rape and assault. In these cases the offenders were arrested by the head chiefs and then handed over to a district officer to be tried by the administration.

At first the administration treated the movement very cautiously. It had soon become apparent that Marching Rule was not a tiny cultist affair confined to a corner of one island. It had spread to many areas and was growing. The power of Marching Rule could not be denied. At a meeting held at Auki on Malaita over 7,000 people assembled and decided that the movement should take over the native courts. At the order of their leaders, whole villages were uprooting themselves and moving down to the coast where Marching Rule 'towns' were being built. These towns were surrounded by pallisades and contained tall look-out towers. Guards were always on duty at the gates and permission had to be obtained for anyone wishing to enter the town. Meeting houses were built at which the men assembled to make

146

great plans for the future. Schools and farms were to be set up, supervised by skilled Europeans who would be fairly paid for their services but would not be the masters. No young men were to leave the area to work on a plantation unless they were paid at least £24 a month and all found, instead of the pre-war 10s a month. This ruling meant that Malaita ceased to be a source of plantation labour as no manager could afford to pay the wages demanded.

There is no doubt that the movement was a nationalist one, but it is equally clear that cargo-cult elements played a part in it. Rows of huts were built to store the gifts that were to arrive from America. Look-outs were appointed to scan the seas for the ships bearing these gifts. One Catholic priest has reported that some of the look-outs would place two bottles to their eyes, simulating the binoculars and field-glasses they had seen American troops use.

The authorities decided that the movement was becoming dangerous. Particular consternation was felt when Vouza, the war hero, emerged as the leading figure of the Guadalcanal Marching Rule section, demanding that he be made paramount chief of the whole island, a position which had never existed in local custom or government administration. People who know Vouza well say that he was never as enthusiastic about the cult as was once thought. It is certain that at meetings with his friends he sometimes seemed to be in two minds about the whole thing. He was, however, an important figure, well known in the United States as the holder of the Silver Star, and a colourful and engaging character. Acting promptly, the authorities sent Vouza to Fiji on a local government course, which effectively removed him from the picture.

Other things were happening, especially on Malaita, to disturb the administration. The SSEM, for instance, was losing a great deal of its authority and islanders who declined to join the movement were not allowed to go to their gardens and were ostracised. No estimate has been made of the number of Malaita people who refused to join, but it is known that Sulufou, the largest of the artificial islands in the Lau Lagoon, remained unaffected. It is certain that at its peak Marching Rule was very strong indeed. Money poured into its coffers; at one time Timothy George collected amost £2,000. People refused to pay taxes. The leaders produced a Marching Rule flag. Adherents of the cult refused to answer census questions, attacked tax-collectors and put up barricades across roads.

For two years the government tried to work with the movement, even declaring some of its aims 'admirable'. When at last it became apparent that there could be no common ground between the government and the movement, district administrators were sent with armed police patrols to visit all the areas known to be affected. The leaders of the movement were told to recant or they would be arrested. Some chiefs did back down; most did not. Nine of the leaders and many followers were arrested. Warships of the British and Australian navies together with a submarine made ostentatious visits to the protectorate, letting themselves be seen off the coasts of the main islands.

The arrests were made in September 1947 and the Marching Rule adherents were tried in Honiara, the new administrative capital. The main charges against the accused islanders were of terrorism and robbery. The trial lasted almost a month. Six men were found not guilty, and the rest were sentenced to terms of imprisonment ranging from one to six years' hard labour. Orders were given to pull down all village fortifications.

Marching Rule did not come to an end with the arrest of its leaders. In some areas it went underground for a time and it was apparent that the cult still had many followers. In 1949 2,000 islanders were serving prison sentences for refusing to pull down fences. New leaders were appointed, with whom the government offered to negotiate, but without effect. An effort was made to take another census but it had to be abandoned because of continuing resistance. In 1950 a district officer's patrol was attacked and a policeman fatally injured. The new leaders of Marching

Rule renamed their organisation the Federal Council. Some of them were arrested.

A SPIRIT OF PROGRESS

In 1952 most of the original Marching Rule leaders had their sentences reduced and were released from prison. The High Commissioner went to Malaita, and some of the islanders who negotiated with him there asked for a 'big man' of their own, and freedom for Malaita. The High Commissioner in turn proposed the formation of a Malaita Council with a big man—a president —elected by the members. The president would have to take a public oath of loyalty to the Queen, recognise the authority of the government and cooperate with the district administrators. This was agreed to and the Malaita Council was formed with Salana Ga'a as its first president. Solomon Islanders were also elected to the Advisory Council, and one of the first four local representatives was Jacob Vouza.

The formation of the Malaita Council did much to settle the island, although elements of Marching Rule continued until at least 1955. In 1951 an official Colonial Office report had said of the efforts to come to terms with the cult: 'Progress, although slow and not spectacular, is being achieved; and while Marching Rule still exists, most of the leaders have now agreed to work with the Administration'. The patience and willingness to compromise shown by the administration during this period did much to resolve the situation, but the movement is still remembered and discussed by islanders as an example of what could be achieved by the people when they put aside their factional differences.

While the post-war administration was struggling to come to terms with the Marching Rule movement it also had the task of rehabilitating the islands after the rigours and excitements of the war period. Genuine efforts appear to have been made to put right previous errors of judgement; more care, for example, was taken in the appointment of headmen so that instead of auto-matically appointing time-expired policemen and the like, leaders were selected for their powers of leadership and their place in the local social hierarchy. Much more emphasis was placed on forma-tion of native councils, thus reducing the numbers of local district headmen. The administration was helped in this by the willing-ness to co-operate displayed on Malaita when it became apparent that the Malaita Council was not a mere constitutional figure-head. In less than two years the council submitted almost seventy resolutions and recommendations to the High Commissioner. A new spirit of progress seemed to be stirring, and efforts were made on both sides. As A. M. Healy has pointed out in his article 'Administration in the British Solomon Islands'.

> It should be emphasised that what assisted the rapid develop-ment of local government in the Solomons was the realisation by many officials with experience elsewhere that the islands were administratively backward, and that the islanders' frustra-tion which resulted had been justified. This led to an atmos-phere of understanding and a readiness for compromise.

Political progress, although slow enough, was far more rapid than advancement in most other areas. There were no war dam-ages or reparations available for anything except government works. Most of the private planters did not return—the mort-gages taken out on their plantations in the 1930s remained and without money it was impossible to clear and restock their planta-tions. It was 1951 before significant copra production got under way once more. Communications with the outside world con-sisted of the shipping service with Australia provided by Burns Philp and a monthly flying-boat service, linking up with Sydney via the New Hebrides and New Caledonia, provided by Trans-Ocean Airways. In 1949 Quantas began a fortnightly air ser-vice via New Guinea, landing at Barakoma and Yandina en route to Honiara.

In 1949 the export of kauri timber from Vanikolo in the east was resumed—before the war there had been quite a sizeable timber concern on the island—but it did not regain its former importance. In 1950 the Auki experimental school was opened. It was later renamed King George VI School and was transferred to Honiara as the government's secondary school. About this time a question on the state of education in the Solomons was asked in the House of Commons and the answer given was to the effect that a Chief Education Officer had just been appointed.

By the 1950s banks and other business ventures were being opened in Honiara. This small and pleasant township had developed from a collection of American buildings close to Point Cruz. The authorities were able to take advantage of the roads, buildings, water and power supplies established by the Americans during the war years. The presence of an airfield just outside the town and wharf facilities actually within its boundaries were two further reasons for the selection of the Honiara site. A narrow coastal plain backed by steep ridges, suitable for residential areas, made the site an attractive one, especially as Honiara was situated in the driest part of the protectorate, with an average annual rainfall of only 80in.

In 1950 the last American troops left Honiara, bringing an end to an association which had lasted in peace and war for eight years. The islanders were sorry to see them go but it may be assumed that the British administration regarded the departure of their erstwhile allies with some relief. In addition to the problems presented by Marching Rule, there were many important matters to be settled, mostly of a cultural and economic nature. In *A Guadalcanal Society*, Ian Hogbin, who had paid a number of visits to the Solomons in the 1930s and 1940s, relates the situation as it affected a part of Guadalcanal he knew well:

By 1945 the traditional headmen had already disappeared. No longer was there any occasion for the great feasts that had enabled men with ambition to rise to the top. The efforts of the missionaries had led to the abandonment of the pagan festivals and also to the stamping out of polygamy, which provided the prospective leader with extra workers; and Government intervention to stop native raiding had meant the end of the offerings to the warrior spirits and of the great overseas trading expeditions. . . . Further, even at that period no member of the older generation was in the position to demand obedience from his juniors. The elders lost their monopoly of the wealth as soon as the youths began earning wages from employment on the plantations, and once a person had become a Christian, he accepted individual responsibility for his actions and ceased to depend on sacrifices carried out by other people.

While this is an accurate summary of the results of island people's contact with expatriates it does perhaps err on the gloomy side. J. L. O. Tedder has pointed out the more attractive aspects of post-war life in the Solomons :

But still the average islander today, even the man who has gained a full primary schooling and returned to his village, spends a comparatively leisured life. He spends some days a week in his garden, goes fishing perhaps one day a week, spends some time repairing his house, doing Council duties or making some copra. He does not work to a clock, his timetable is flexible and when he wishes he can take a holiday. His life is that of the independent man-of-means.

MORE BREAKAWAYS

Not long after the problems of Marching Rule had been more or less satisfactorily resolved, a similar sort of organisation came into being. This was the Moro movement, which had its beginnings on Guadalcanal in 1957 when a prophet called Moro began preaching that there should be a return to the old custom ways. Some of his supporters threatened a police patrol and were sent to prison, Moro himself, a former labourer, receiving a sentence of three months' duration. Moro claimed to have been visited in a dream by a spirit who told him that he was to become leader of the Marau-Hauba peoples on that part of the coast of Guadalcanal. Moro's term of imprisonment made something of a martyr of him and after his release the movement spread rapidly along the coast of Guadalcanal.

Rumours spread that the 'black Americans' were backing Moro and that ship-loads of goods would be arriving for his followers. The movement became known as the Moro Custom Company and began to advocate complete independence from the government. Large sums of money were collected and a communal plantation established. Davenport and Coker, who studied the movement at first hand, estimate that by 1964 the movement was exerting a strong influence over at least half of Guadalcanal. With the bitter lessons of Marching Rule in mind the administration treated Moro with great caution. Davenport and Coker (see bibliography) quote from an address of Moro's to the Acting High Commissioner in 1964 :

> Tomorrow the peoples of Moro's Custom Company will be looking forward. The principle [aid] from civilisation is money. We are now starting with our fashion of marketing. We realise that money makes better education, better business, and better development of civilisation. Without money we can do nothing. Money makes things possible.
>
> We have been waiting for many years. Since the missions came to the Solomons, we have not seen any change from our old habit of living except the changing of faith and a bit of education.
>
> The traders and the Government also came and live in the Solomons for many years, but there has been no changes made. Only during the last few years when the Government set up a school at Auki in the Malaita District, which is now known as King George VI School, and then began to take over the education from the missions. Sir, the Solomons should have been well off if schools started right at the years of the arrival of the white man in the Solomons.
>
> Your Excellency, we are [very] suspicious. The Europeans in the time past seemed to rob our lands. Some of our lands were bought with empty bottles. Today, as we can see the boundaries of the land of Honiara is still moving into the lands of the natives. . . .

Moro was the son of a local big man and inherited some of the custom magic of his father, including the power to calm stormy

153

seas. After working as a labourer for the Americans on Tulagi and in the gardens of Honiara he fell ill in 1956. He claims that his friends thought that he was dead and even made arrangements to bury him. During his coma Moro experienced several visitations, which he later discussed with a fellow-villager, David Valusa, a schoolteacher. He, being able to speak and write English, wrote down Moro's ideas. Within a comparatively short time the movement was well organised and was drawing adherents from other Guadalcanal villages. In 1965 Moro and some of his followers went to Honiara and offered the district commissioner £2,000 for their independence, although Moro has since claimed that the money was intended for the High Commissioner to help them obtain a better life. The request was denied and Moro and his men were asked to go back to their homes. Since then the movement has continued to attract adherents and seems to be a force to be reckoned with in the future development of the Solomons; expatriate missionaries of several denominations declare that it was still actively strong in 1972.

Another movement to attract a great deal of attention in the islands was the formation of the Christian Fellowship Church which broke away from the Methodists in the west in 1960. The leader of the schism was Silas Eto and he took about 20 villages and some 3,000 people with him. Eto had been a mission teacher and had been highly regarded by the expatriate missionary Goldie who had even allowed him to go back to his own village after his training period, a most unusual concession. During the war he came into contact with many American troops in the area and was impressed by some of the ideas put to him by these soldiers, particularly the coloured ones, who were Mormons and Jehovah's Witnesses. In 1949 Eto was advocating changes in the Solomons, particularly the union of all churches in one denomination, one trading company for the whole protectorate, and better relationships between the missions and the government. Then—about ten years later—he seems to have lost faith in his ability to achieve anything from within the church. Accordingly he led his breakaway movement in the area of the Roviana and Maravo lagoons, giving himself the title of 'Holy Mama' and calling his church the Christian Fellowship Church.

RESULTS OF PATIENCE

Constitutional development was taking place at the same time as these political and religious upheavals. In 1953 the headquarters of the Western Pacific High Commission moved to Honiara from Fiji, which meant that the High Commissioner took up residence in the Solomons. In 1960 the advisory council was replaced by an executive council and a legislative council, and local councils, although more strongly supported in some areas than in others, continued to flourish. In 1963 a local government ordinance provided wider powers for them, including the levying of rates, and also decreed the election of members by universal adult suffrage in place of the former nomination.

By the 1960s the results of a great deal of patient work on the part of both government and islanders were beginning to be seen. Financial grants made by Great Britain enabled specific schemes of development to be carried out. The increase in the number of children being educated and the improved health and consequent annual increase in population were also landmarks in postwar development. The multiplication of government departments and their expatriate personnel were regarded by some islanders as a necessary step in order to carry out the various projects being launched; others thought that the administrative sections were in some areas becoming top-heavy, especially as it was not until the 1970s that islanders began to occupy some of the senior posts in these departments.

In 1961 the first local trades union was formed in the shape of the British Solomon Islands Union, taking its members from port and plantation workers. At this time the total labour force was estimated to be in the region of 8,000 and the average wage of a labourer was £6 10s a month. Four years later the union was involved in a strike for better wages and conditions. A march through Honiara became unruly and the police dispersed the members with tear gas. Afterwards the union languished and was wound up.

Young Solomon Islanders were beginning to wonder about the future—when would independence be granted the islands and what would the results of this independence be? The thoughts of some of the islanders were summed up by Francis Bugotu in 1967, writing in C. E. Fox's *The Story of the Solomons*:

> Good government takes a long time to evolve as we learn when we study Constitutional changes and developments in other countries like Britain and Australia. Whatever form our future government takes it must be rooted in the Solomon Islanders's way of life to be good and successful. Stable government cannot be bought or copied. We cannot copy from Britain or any other country, because what is copied is not understood and understanding must be our aim at the base. We must learn and study governmental systems of Britain and other countries of the world, but ours must evolve. It must evolve from the Solomon Islands thought and ideals, with general understanding of the world situation and our relation to it.

One of the most pressing problems that Solomon Islanders will have to face with the approach of independence is the lack of mutual trust between the different islanders and between Melanesians and the minority groups. An example of this was given by D. G. Cochrane, a former administrative officer in the group, writing in *Oceania* in an article entitled 'Racialism in the Pacific'. He described how he tried to persuade the Polynesians of Tikopia to join more closely with the other islands:

> In 1967 I had to explain to the chiefs why Government wanted the Tikopia to participate in the Legislative Council. In my preliminary conversation with the Ariki Tafua he expressed himself graciously though patronisingly on the subject of Melanesian polititics. When I mentioned what the Government

Page 157 Different types: *(top left)* pipe player at festival; *(top right)* young man of Lord Howe Island; *(below left)* old man of Santa Isabel; *(below right)* Charles Woodford, first resident commissioner of the Solomons

Page 158 Houses: *(above)* homes on legs at Port Adam, Malaita. The legs protect the houses against floods and allow shelter for canoes; *(below)* homes on an artificial island in Langa Langa Lagoon, Malaita

had in mind the atmosphere became more chilly. The chiefs maintained that the black men were numerically superior, they knew nothing of the customs of Tikopia, and if any decisions were to be made they would favour their own kind. I was informed that if I was a friend of Tikopia I would tell Government that it was not to put them in with the black men. In 1964 I had had to try to persuade the Gilbertese at Wagina to come under the Choiseul Island local council, and they had used the same arguments.

Such mutual distrust is still felt today. It is to be hoped that with improved communications, better educational facilities and a genuine desire to make the best of conditions, an atmosphere of co-operation will somehow come about.

7   THE ISLANDS TODAY

TOWARDS SELF-GOVERNMENT

IT is generally assumed that internal self-government will be
granted to the Solomons some time between 1975 and 1980,
although no official pronouncement has been made on the
subject. At the moment the protectorate is administered by the
High Commissioner for the Western Pacific, who is appointed
from London. The work of the central government in the Solomons is to look after the finance and administration, education,
medical work, police, lands, trade and communications, and
generally to govern the protectorate. This is carried out by a
number of government departments, staffed at the higher levels
mostly by expatriates, who are responsible to the High Commissioner. The islands are divided for administrative purposes into
four districts, each under a district commissioner assisted by one
or more district officers.

With some outstanding exceptions an attitude of benevolent
paternalism, at odds with the growing demand for independence,
prevails. Many islanders feel that no great sense of urgency is
displayed by most government departments and that a number
of the more highly paid civil servants are more concerned with
hanging on to their jobs than in implementing the localisation
policies which are issued from time to time. Certainly, in spite
of such localisation policies, there are more expatriates working
for government now—some 400 of them—than at any other
time. A large proportion of senior administrators and depart-
mental heads are former European civil servants released from
African states as they achieved independence.

160

In the last decade the constitution has undergone a number of changes, with more and more power being placed in the hands of elected members who are now in the majority in the governing council. Until 1960 an advisory council composed of official and non-official members assisted the High Commissioner. In 1960 nominated legislative and executive councils were established. Four years later provision was made for a new constitution. The main change lay in the fact that eight of the ten unofficial members were to be elected, not nominated. In 1965 a general election was held. The legislative council subsequently consisted of three ex-officio members, eight official members, eight elected and two nominated unofficial members. The executive council at this time consisted of ten members, appointed by the High Commissioner from legislative council members. This establishment of a governing body with elected islanders representing their districts was a considerable step forward in the development of the Solomons.

There were a number of teething troubles. The meetings of the legislative council in the council chamber at Honiara were so arranged at one time that the elected members sat on one side while the nominated ex-officio heads of government departments and senior civil servants sat on the other side facing them. As most of the elected members were islanders and all the ex-officio members were expatriates there was felt to be an aura of discrimination. This was heightened by the fact that all debates were conducted in English, while many of the elected members were more at home in pidgin. The elected members were also unfamiliar with procedural matters and were not always able to pin down official members at question time. All members had to wear suits, and this some of the younger people felt to be unnecessary and pretentious in the climate of the Solomons.

At the next general election, in 1967, arrangements were made to elect fourteen members instead of eight. Polling took place in May and June and the resulting council consisted of three ex-officio members—the Chief Secretary, the Attorney-General and the Financial Secretary—up to twelve public service members and the fourteen elected members. There was provision for up to two additional nominated members. The executive council consisted of eight members appointed by the High Commissioner from legislative council members, their function being to advise the High Commissioner on important decisions.

At the end of 1968 a further effort was made to construct a legislative and administrative system which would best enable the elected members to express themselves. This constituted a departure from the Westminster model in that it proposed the formation of a single council supported by executive committees. There was to be an increase in the number of elected members from fourteen to seventeen, and an official representation of three ex-officio and not more than six public service members. This new constitution, generally accepted as a far-seeing and genuine attempt to adapt democratic government to traditional Melanesian ways, came into force in 1970.

It is too early to assess the working of this constitution and indeed to make any forecast about the political future of the Solomons. As yet there are no political parties, although several have been mooted, and no apparent public demand for any, though this may change with the first major influx of Solomon Island graduates from the University of the South Pacific and the University of Papua–New Guinea. It is not possible to make any generalisations about the type of men being elected to the new governing council. In 1972 only two seats were occupied by Europeans, one a minister of the Melanesian Mission and the other a plantation owner, both residents of the Solomons for some years. The rest of the elected members varied greatly in background, from old-time local headmen to young, educated former government officers. It is a fair assumption that a man with many relations in a certain area would have a good chance of being elected in that area, and that the 'big man' system also has its effect on votes. Local residents also consider that on part of Guadalcanal the candidate favoured by the Moro movement would be sure of a large bloc of votes, and the same would apply to anyone supported by the Christian Fellowship Church in parts of the western district.

A number of the elected members of the governing council were not slow in expressing disenchantment with their lot. They were by no means all in favour of the committee system established. There are five committees, approximating to ministries : Natural Resources, Communications and Finance, Works, Education and Social Welfare, Health and Internal Affairs. Each is staffed by elected members with one of their number as chairman, and with a government officer in attendance. It was not long before some members were complaining that the civil servants were really running the committees and that the elected members were having very little say in what went on. One elected member went so far as to put a placard in the back window of his car which read 'Rubber Stamp', indicating his displeasure with the system under which he claimed he was allowed mainly to approve bills already prepared.

The elected members themselves came under fire from their constituents during the early sessions of the first governing council, particularly when they voted themselves an increase in salary. Under the new system the chairman of a committee received $A5,427 a year and an ordinary member received $A3,400 a year. A greater furore was caused, however, when the government began to look for ways of increasing revenue. In 1970 the Solomons received from Great Britain a grant-in-aid of $A2·3 million. In addition it also received capital aid of $A2·6 million. It was an avowed policy of the government to try and achieve some measure of financial independence hand-in-hand with the quest for political independence. Therefore, to prevent the unnecessary importation of food into the protectorate and in order to give a boost to the local rice-growing industry a heavy duty was placed on Australian rice, which then retailed at about $A7 a sack while the local variety cost only $4·50. Unfortunately the local rice was not at all popular with islanders, many claiming

163

that it was inferior to the Australian variety. As rice, especially for town-dwellers, is a staple item of diet, the increase in price was greatly resented. The sale of the locally produced rice did not increase markedly and the elected members were reviled for allowing the price increase to be pushed through in the governing council.

An even greater controversy early in the life of the first governing council was caused by an agreement signed by the government with the Taiyo Fishing Company of Japan, by which the company was allowed to undertake an eighteen-month fishing survey of the potential catch in Solomon waters. Six boats were to be allowed to fish up to 500yd off the shores of the islands. When the Japanese boats actually appeared off the coast a storm of protest went up from the people and reverberated in the council chamber. David Kausimae, Chairman of the Natural Resources Committee and an elected member for a Malaita constituency, was strongly criticised for giving way to the administrators. A number of elected members joined in the attack on Kausimae. The sea, one of them stated, was traditionally the garden of the Solomons; the Japanese would denude the sea of fish and the people would starve.

Seldom had the elected members been so united on anything. The administrators were accused of not giving the matter sufficient publicity before the agreement had been signed. Jonathan Fifi, another elected member from Malaita and a former participant in the Marching Rule movement, said that feelings ran as high over the Japanese fishing vessels as they had done during the time of Marching Rule.

It was pointed out by the Financial Secretary that whether or not the fishing industry came to the Solomons was up to the governing council; they could vote against it if they wanted to. However, if they did reject the industry they were turning away a possible annual income of a quarter of a million dollars. David Kausimae also spoke on the matter and said that he had agreed to the trial survey because he wanted to see the Solomons inde-

pendent by 1975 when the country would need all the revenue
it could get. It was agreed finally that the fishing vessels should
be restricted to waters at least three miles off the coast, but even
this did not satisfy many members, who wanted a twelve-mile
limit imposed.

A large number of electors felt that their representatives had
let them down over the Taiyo Fishing Company case. In other
matters, however, elected members to the governing council have
displayed independence, rejecting a number of motions prepared
by the administration. A bill making it compulsory for Solomon
Islanders to pay for medical treatment at clinics was defeated,
and some members, Peter Salaka representing Honiara prominent
among them, have been pressing for increased localisation of
government posts.

In addition to the central government, nearly all islands or sub-
districts now have local councils which look after or improve
administrative services, communications, rural health clinics,
schools, water supplies, market centres, and so on. For this work
the local councils obtain their revenue from a basic rate which is
paid annually by every able-bodied man. The rate varies with
different councils, but on average is about five dollars a year.
Councils also get money from the sale of dog licences, hawkers'
and bakers' licences, and so on. All local councils are wholly
elected by secret ballot with universal adult suffrage, as are the
elected members of the governing council.

The powers and efficiency of the different councils vary. The
one on Malaita is very powerful, while a united council is being
formed for the western district which should have a great deal of
authority. In some areas council members complain that the district commissioners are slow to hand over authority to them and
prefer to maintain the 'old colonial' policy of the district commissioner as autocrat in his part of the protectorate. Complaints
have been made that no provision yet exists whereby councils
can take over from district commissioners.

In a country of scattered islands in which communications are

165

notoriously difficult and where many people have little or no education, it is difficult to judge the amount of interest in and understanding of government in the Solomons. District officers tour and talk to the people about constitutional development, and the local radio service has broadcast a few pidgin talks about it. In the 1970 governing council elections 55·40 per cent of the 51,904 registered voters went to the polls. The proportion of voters bothering to use their votes at local council elections varies greatly from district to district. On the island of Savo practically every adult votes, while at one Honiara election only six people turned up at the polls.

About 50 per cent of the children of the Solomons get some form of education, although for most of them it consists only of a few years of schooling at an elementary level in the village. There are some 400 primary schools, 6 secondary schools, a technical institute and a teachers' training college.

The village school at which the average child receives two or three years of education usually consists of a one-room leaf building, constructed by the teacher and the men of the village, who also make the crude wooden desks. The school is often presided over by a villager who himself has probably had only seven years' education and has undergone no form of teacher-training. If he is lucky he will have a blackboard, some chalk, a textbook or two and some exercise books. There will probably be a radio set on which the children can listen to some of the schools broadcasts which are transmitted by the Education Department for three hours every morning.

Occasionally the village teacher will be a dedicated man with a sense of vocation. Only too often he will have been delegated the post by his fellow villagers or by his church because he is the only man in the area to have had any sort of education himself. Most of the teaching is done in the vernacular, or in pidgin if

166

the teacher comes from other parts. English is taught by means of a method known as the Tate Oral English Course and is centred around a set of textbooks and daily conversation lessons provided by the schools broadcasting service for standards 1–5 in the junior primary schools. A smattering of arithmetic is taught and a great deal of religious instruction given, varying in content according to the denomination of the village concerned. School begins at about eight in the morning and usually finishes for the day at noon.

Education is not compulsory and is largely in the hands of the churches, although lately local councils have started to take over the primary schools on some islands. The government is responsible for King George VI Secondary School, the Technical Institute and the British Solomons Training College.

The junior primary schools in the villages nominally take in children between the ages of 7 and 11. Senior primary schools take in the 11–15 age-range, in standards 5–7. There are also a number of full-range schools teaching standards 1–7. Full-range and senior primary schools are staffed largely by trained teachers and are usually boarding establishments situated away from villages. Such schools have to be largely self-supporting and most afternoons are occupied by teachers and students in working in the school gardens, growing food for themselves.

Efforts are being made to bring down the age of senior primary students so that those who go on to secondary education may do so at the age of fourteen, but some pupils at secondary schools may be twenty years old and even more. Entry to secondary education is competitive by means of various tests, and only a small proportion of candidates are successful. In 1970, 329 boys and 123 girls of all the standard 7 leavers managed to get to one of the six secondary schools in the Solomons.

The government policy with regard to education is to provide secondary education for those able to benefit from it in order to train tradesmen, craftsmen and schoolteachers for the needs of the Solomons; and so to orientate the curriculum of primary schools that the overwhelming majority of children who must return to village life are prepared to do so and take their place in village society.

In practice this policy is running into a great deal of trouble. It is felt in some circles that the concentration of money and resources on producing an educational élite capable of taking over responsible jobs in government and commerce is a mistaken one. It has been pointed out that fifty children out of every hundred get no education at all and that many of the remainder are being badly taught under poor conditions. King George VI School, on the other hand, has cost over $A1 million dollars to build and takes a great deal to maintain in order to educate 300 or so pupils. The official attitude is that trained manpower is necessary, that there is little time left before self-determination in which to produce it, and that secondary education must therefore be given a larger share of the cake.

The government is also doing its best to produce trained teachers. A two-year course is provided at the British Solomons Training College, which also runs a six-month intensive course for untrained teachers.

In 1940, in his report on a survey of education in the Solomons, William Groves pointed out the way that education must go for the vast majority of islanders :

It is apparent to anyone with a knowledge of the Protectorate that the natural basis for native development lies in the socially-integrated rural community organisation and life. And any educational scheme designed to develop the mass of the people and strengthen them in their community life, must recognise this; it must focus upon rural interests and activities, and relate itself to the needs of hamlet and village.

It must aim at the improvement of rural community standards —in health, food, housing, care of children, moral life, status of women, and in mental outlook. It must seek to enrich and stabilise native life in its natural rural setting, and to adjust its organisation to modern conditions and needs. . . .

The first step will be to secure the best of the native human material offering, train it for leadership along the desired lines, strengthening it in its attachment to rural life (not moulding it into half-baked European form); and give these leaders scope for the exercise of their leadership qualities and the application of their special training, under sympathetic European direction and support. 'The best of human material' does not necessarily mean the best according to European school ideas.

Nothing that has been written about education in the Solomons over the past thirty years could surpass this summary of the educational needs of Solomon Islanders. It would be foolish to pretend that attempts to put this policy into effect have met with spectacular success. The drift away from the villages to the town is increasing. Those children who leave senior primary school after seven years of education and return to the village sometimes feel that rural life no longer has much to offer them; they feel cheated of a secondary education and sometimes consider that they have been shown a brief glimpse of something better only to have the door slammed in their faces. This applies to many of the secondary-educated children who want to find work in Honiara and only reluctantly go back to their homes. Standards required for the sought-after government posts in the town and district stations are steadily rising as the number of educated school-leavers increase. Once a standard 7 primary school-leaver could enter government service; now a minimum of two years of secondary education is required, and this may well be raised to four or five years of secondary education. Today, as in 1940, any scheme of education for the Solomons has to take into account the pressing needs of the vast majority of school-leavers who must go back to their home villages.

In a survey conducted for the South Pacific Commission by Karel Meijs in 1954 it was estimated that between 70 and 80 per cent of the population within the orbit of the missions was literate, and this figure would probable be higher today. Most people are literate in the vernacular rather than in English, the missions having translated hymns, prayer books and parts of the Bible into island languages.

There would be little or no education in the Solomons today had it not been for the pioneering work of the different missions and for their continuing efforts to educate islanders. Perhaps the Anglican Melanesian Mission has the widest sphere of influence. In 1850 Bishop Selwyn took a small number of island boys to St John's College in Auckland, the headquarters of the mission, where they were taught in company with English and Maori boys. In 1859 a school for Melanesian boys only was established under Lonsdale Pritt at St Andrew's, Kohimarama, and trans-ferred to Norfolk Island in 1867 where it continued as the main school of the mission, with a roll of some 200 boys, until 1919. One of the pioneers of this school was Dr Codrington, an early authority on ethnography and linguistics in Melanesia. The medium of instruction in the school was Mota, the official mis-sion language of New Hebridean origin, but even at this early stage English figured as a school subject. Other subjects included reading, writing, arithmetic, singing, farming and carpentry. Usually pupils remained at the school for six years, although some, with breaks for holidays, were in residence for up to twelve years. Returning to the islands, these boys established schools in their own villages, the first being in San Cristobal, Ulawa, South Malaita and Gela in 1865; others were started rather later, on Santa Isabel and Savo, and in about 1900 in Guadalcanal and north Malaita. When in 1919 the Norfolk Island school was closed, some thirty village schools had been established in the Solomons and the mission claims that all people in the Christian villages were literate in their own language.

Slowly a number of senior schools under expatriate missionary headmasters like Dr Welchman and Dr Fox were established in the islands, and in about 1925 it was decided that English should replace Mota as the means of instruction at these. By the outbreak of the war in the Solomons the mission had also established a small number of 'district' schools—regional boarding institutions offering a slightly higher standard of education than the village schools, with educated islanders as teachers. This development was continued after the war. Another post-war development was the establishment of native junior schools to feed the senior school of the mission, Pawa. The mission did not neglect the education of girls although originally only girls betrothed to the male students were allowed to attend the Norfolk Island school, this being insisted upon by their parents. Gradually schools for girls were established by the mission in the islands.

Roman Catholic sponsored education really began in the Solo-mons at the end of the nineteenth century. In 1899 some thirty-five young islanders were being educated at the mission station of Rua Sura, off the coast of Guadalcanal, and in the same year another mission station was opened at Avu Avu on the main island. Here, despite the opposition of parents, the arrival of labour-recruiting vessels and the shortage of food, a school was established. In 1900 the Marist Fathers of Nila in the Short-land Islands began their first school in the western district.

By 1928 boarding schools for boys and girls were functioning and continued until the Japanese invasion in 1942. In this year two European priests and two sisters were executed by the Japanese at Ruavatu Mission. At Marau, which was the mission's most promising pre-war educational venture, a senior training institution was established in 1936 with an expatriate priest in charge and forty boys in residence. Two years later, in 1938, there arrived three qualified teachers belonging to the Marist Brothers. The school aimed to produce a higher-calibre native teacher and leader for village and station work by adapting its work to local conditions and relating its programme to native life. With the Japanese invasion the school ceased to function, but was re-established later at Tenaru, some fourteen miles east of Honiara. The mission also has schools in Malaita including the main station at Buma, and at Wanoni Bay on San Cristo-bal.

The main sphere of influence of the United Church is in the western district. In 1910, the first trained teacher Miss M. Davies came to Roviana, where she stayed until 1914; she was followed by other sisters, not all of whom were qualified teachers. In 1922 the first male trained teacher came to Roviana from Fiji and, on his departure six years later, a second one came for a further period of three years. In 1924, a second qualified woman teacher, Miss L. M. Jones, came to Roviana, and during the course of her twenty-five years' service brought about many improvements in the primary schools of the headquarters station. The Pacific war seriously disrupted the mission's activities also and the majority of schools established had to be closed. Some of the best students, however, were sent to the Melanesian Mission senior school at Pawa, and a few to Fiji and Tonga for specialist training as radio operators. After the war schools were gradually reopened and today there are some 300 United Church teachers at schools in the western district.

The Seventh Day Adventist Mission set up district boarding schools shortly after its establishment at Gizo in 1914. From these, after a period of two or three years, islanders went out to teach as best they might in the villages of the area. In turn, pupils from the village schools came to the district schools, and the best of these were sent to a central school established in 1934 at Batuna in the Marovo Lagoon of the western district.

Co-education was the practice from the first in the Adventist schools. Before the war Marovo was used as the medium of instruction (as Roviana had been used by the Methodists), but this was replaced after the war by English. In 1951 special textbooks for island schools were introduced and in 1957 the syllabus was revised. In 1947 the central school established at Batuna was transferred to Betikama on Guadalcanal, and five years later a second central school was established at Kukudu, on the island of Kolombangara in the west.

The first South Sea Evangelical Mission school was started on a Malaita plantation soon after 1904. Pidgin was the language used and the children were taught writing, simple number work and singing. This school was later transferred to the mission headquarters at One Pusu. The next decade saw a considerable extension of the mission's work with the translation of the New Testament into the Malu language, and the Catechism into the languages of the districts to which the mission penetrated. In many villages reading in the vernacular was taught phonetically by means of 'syllable books' and a short time each day was devoted to the reading of simple English. In the 1930s great advances were made; numbers at One Pusu (and these included married couples and single men) rose to more than 180 and the course lasted for up to four years. This period saw the beginning of schools for children run by the islanders themselves, some boarding and some day schools. Teaching in these schools was in the vernacular.

The war and then the Marching Rule movement were disturbing times for the schools of this Mission. On Malaita many of the leaders of Marching Rule were SSEM teachers and pastors who broke away from the church. Parents discouraged their children from attending school, and in the end the mission altered its policy and concentrated on the training of pastors and evangelists rather than teachers. But after 1954 schools gradually re-opened and in 1960 the mission reviewed its education policy once more and started to bring in expatriate teachers, particularly from Australia and New Zealand.

Government interest in education began in 1946 with the establishment of a small Department of Education. This was increased in size in 1952 when grants-in-aid to the value of about $A12,000 were made. Today, in addition to its responsibility for much of the education at tertiary level, the government is also responsible for an educational broadcasting service and provides district education officers to inspect schools, run courses and generally assist the mission and council schools. Schools recognised as having reached a certain standard of efficiency and with a proportion of trained staff are termed 'scheduled' and receive a government grant. The government also pays a substantial proportion of the salaries of trained teachers, the remainder being found by the mission or council concerned.

PROBLEMS IN AGRICULTURE

The economy of the Solomon Islands is based on its copra production of some 24,000 tons a year. The total amount of land planted with coconuts is not accurately known, although about 22,000 acres, producing rather less than half of the annual output, are planted by European-owned estates, the largest of which is Lever Brothers' Pacific Plantations with its headquarters at Yandina in the Russells, where they maintain a joint research scheme with the Department of Agriculture. The remainder of the annual output is provided by Solomon Islanders. The Department of Agriculture assists indigenous farmers with a scheme of planting subsidies and professional advice from touring agriculture officers and field assistants. Improved transport and marketing facilities will have to be provided if farmers are to be encouraged to increase their production. The quality of plantation copra is, however, much higher than that of village copra. About 77 per cent of plantation copra is graded as first-class, while only 39 per cent of village-produced copra is of the highest grade. The copra production of the Solomons makes up about 81 per cent of the protectorate's domestic exports and about 1 per cent of the world's production, with the United Kingdom, Australia and Japan as its biggest customers. The Solomon Islands Copra Board regulates buying prices at the three main ports of Gizo, Honiara and Yandina. Prices paid by the Board after a slump in 1972 were: $A70 a ton for first grade, $A66 a ton for second grade and $A56 a ton for third grade copra. Most villagers, however, sell their copra to Chinese middlemen who send their boats round the islands, and it has been estimated that islanders receive an average of 45 per cent of the Copra Board's buying price from the middlemen. Co-operative societies are try-

Page 175 Wild life: *(above)* baby crocodiles found and nurtured by a Guadal-canal plantation owner; *(below)* Reef heron, one of the birds to be seen on the shores of the Solomons

Page 176 (above) Cormorants on the island of Rennell; (below) digging for mega-pode eggs on Savo

ing to cut out these middlemen, but handle only some 11 per cent of the total village production.

A major agricultural development in 1971 was the establishment on the Guadalcanal Plains of an 8,000 acre oil-palm estate. This was financed by the Commonwealth Development Corporation and it is intended to make oil palm the country's second largest agricultural export industry. Also on the Guadalcanal Plains some 3,000 tons of rice are being produced annually by a commercial firm, Guadalcanal Plains Ltd. This rice is purchased and consumed locally.

In the 1950s extensive efforts were made to introduce cocoa as a major crop, but these did not succeed, to the indignation of a number of Malaita farmers who had been persuaded to give over much of their land to the experiment. Between 90 and 100 tons a year are currently being produced.

Cattle, although primarily kept for brushing plantations, that is for keeping the undergrowth at bay, are becoming increasingly important as a source of food. It is hoped that the increase in local beef production over the next decade will help reduce imports of fresh meat. There are also about 20,000 pigs in the Solomons, and it is estimated that in the villages the consumption of pork averages out at between 5 and 6lb per head per year. In villages, chickens, ducks and geese are kept and some goats are bred. As has already been mentioned, the main subsistence crops are taro, yams and sweet potatoes. Cash and subsistence cropping are closely related, but among those crops grown mainly for sale in the market or even mainly for export are chillies, ginger, limes and tobacco. In his article, 'The Solomon Islands —An Emerging Cash Economy' (see bibliography), J. L. O. Tedder describes the ways in which the government is seeking to assist the small farmer—by publications and other information services, advisory and research staff, provision of loans, sale of seednuts at reduced prices, etc—but goes on to point out that in addition to the shortage of good roads and harbours, and the unreliability of shipping services, there still remain many prob-

L

lems to overcome in the development of agriculture in the Solomons, especially in the production of copra :

> Yet problems still remain; groves are still left uncleared, nuts are still left lying on the ground to sprout, seed nuts planted in seed beds are never planted out, new plantings become overgrown, and copra is still made badly and so rejected. In other words here is a source of cash which is not being used to full advantage due, perhaps, to several factors including a greater propensity for leisure than for cash.

TRANSPORT DIFFICULTIES

Solair, the Solomon Islands Airways—a subsidiary of Macair, the Papua–New Guinea airline—operates services to many of the islands. The two aircraft, a Beechcraft Baron and a Britten-Norman Islander together with another Beechcraft on lease, carry over 10,000 passengers a year, well over half of them private passengers and the remainder government officers. Fares are based on the rate of 8·9 cents per seat per kilometre travelled. The international airfield at Honiara is in the process of being equipped for night operations. District airstrips at Auki, Parasi, Kirakira, Yandina, Sege, Choiseul Bay, Munda, Santa Cruz, Barakoma, Nusatupe, Ballalae, Rennell and Bellona are well tended, but two strips on the weather coast of Guadalcanal—Marau and Avuavu—sometimes give cause for concern, while the strip at Mono in the west has from time to time been closed because it has been neglected and allowed to become overgrown.

A transport survey conducted by two experts from London considered the feasibility of introducing hovercraft, hydrofoils and helicopters to the islands, but decided that costs and technical difficulties weighed heavily against them. Floatplanes have also been considered. The Missionary Aviation Society flew down a demonstration Cessna 180 floatplane from West Irian and carried out a series of flights, landing a number of times in bays and harbours. The drawbacks to this type of aircraft were shown to be the lack of suitable safe anchorages and landing places in many parts of the protectorate, and also the relatively low carrying capacity of floatplanes. On the other hand the demonstration Cessna impressed many onlookers, and it may be that difficulties will be overcome.

Aeroplanes, however, can move only a fraction of the passengers and goods transported in the Solomons. The vast majority of people and the bulk of material are moved by ship. The government-run Marine Department operates some forty ships with a gross registered tonnage in excess of 1,500. These vessels vary considerably, as do the ships operated by commercial concerns, but for administrative purposes they are divided by the Marine Department into five main categories. These are (a) foreign-going, that is licensed to travel outside the Solomons; (b) outer-island vessels, licensed to travel anywhere in the Solomons, usually over 60ft in length, carrying some twenty-five to thirty passengers; (c) inner-island vessels licensed to travel among the main groups of islands but not to the outer eastern islands or the remote Polynesian outliers—these are usually between 45 and 60ft in length and carry about twenty passengers; (d) intermediate vessels licensed to travel among the main groups of islands, about 40ft long and carrying ten or twelve passengers; (e) coastal vessels carrying between three and six passengers and not venturing more than five miles from land at any point unless escorted by another larger vessel.

It is the duty of the vessels of the Marine Department to provide for the shipping needs of the government. This can include carrying government officers on their tours of the islands, bringing in schoolchildren to the capital at the beginning of term and taking them back to their homes in the holidays, and carrying government freight—materials for the building of wharfs, clinics, airstrips, and so on. It is the policy of the department not to take private freight if there are commercial vessels available for this purpose.

The administration of the Marine Department is in the hands of a few expatriate officials, but with one exception the men in charge of the ships are all Solomon Islanders, men who have qualified at the local marine training school and obtained their practical experience in the marine fleet. The one vessel captained by an expatriate is the largest in the department, the *Belama*, built in 1958, with a gross tonnage of 285. Her cargo capacity is 85 tons and she can carry eighty passengers, the majority of them on deck although there are four cabins each capable of taking two or three people. The cabin service includes meals prepared by the staff of the vessel. At the other end of the scale the government owns coast-hugging vessels such as the *Tanabule* and other 'T'-class ships (gross tonnage 9) capable of carrying only eight passengers.

While most of the vessels belonging to the Marine Department are based on Honiara, a number are allocated to district work and based, for example, at Santa Isabel; government officers who make their way to this island by a larger vessel may transfer to the *Tanabule* to go round the coast of the island.

The Marine Department and the District Commissioners issue monthly shipping schedules for the vessels in the fleet, and government officers wishing to visit one of the villages en route book passages on the appropriate ship, telling the booking clerk where they wish to be dropped and whether they want another scheduled vessel to pick them up further along the coast. Non-government passengers may also book passages on these ships; most Solomon Islanders travel as deck passengers, sleeping on the crowded decks on mats, as cabin passages are very expensive by comparison and the accommodation far from luxurious—usually just a bunk in a hot and crowded box.

Travelling by ship in the Solomons, with the possible exception of the *Belama*, is not usually a comfortable business. The ships are crowded with deck passengers, often bringing pigs, chickens and dogs with them. More often than not the seas are rough and most ships pitch badly and move very slowly towards the eventual destination. Some of the medium-sized vessels have cooking facilities but it is difficult to maintain one's balance and fry an egg in inclement conditions, even if the desire to do so is there. Most passengers reach their destinations with great relief and are glad to be rowed ashore in the ship's dinghy or to transfer to a canoe and reach land in that way.

About 200 vessels operate in Solomon waters, most of them privately owned. The missions own their own ships, and a number of plantation owners also possess vessels which transport copra and other goods. A few local firms, such as Markworth Shipping, Melanchine Shipping and Kwan How Yuan Company, own small fleets of up to half a dozen vessels which take passengers and trade goods round the protectorate and often purchase copra for the return journey, but many vessels are owner-run. The Chinese are particularly prominent in this as in most commercial ventures.

The most heavily frequented shipping routes are those between Guadalcanal and Malaita, Guadalcanal and the Floridas, and Guadalcanal and Santa Isabel, all relatively short distances. It is still difficult to get to the remoter regions of the east and west and there is often a long wait for ships going to those parts. The first regular commercial shipping service was instituted by the Markworth Shipping Company in 1966, when the government gave a boost to commercial shipping by largely withdrawing from freight transport, in which it had been competing with commercial interests. The Markworth vessels are not large, the biggest is about 40 tons, but they do provide regular services between Honiara and parts of the west, while Melanchine Shipping runs a regular twice-weekly service between Honiara and Auki on Malaita. In 1968 a transport survey revealed that while shipping routes and services were improving there were still important gaps, especially between New Georgia and Choiseul in the west, between Guadalcanal and Rennell and Bellona in the central district, and between San Cristobal and the eastern outer islands.

There is a great shortage of shipping for all purposes in the Solomons. Only 9 vessels out of the 200 have over 50 tons carrying capacity and only 4 can carry more than 50 people. Most of the vessels are of conventional wooden construction. Four are built of steel—the *Belama*, two government-owned landing craft and the commercially owned *Warroo II*. The fifteen vessels owned by the churches are fully engaged in mission work and while the three major commercial shipping organisations operate scheduled runs the majority of owner-run vessels, usually cutter boats operating from Honiara or Gizo in the west make their way around the islands in a more haphazard manner, calling in at some thirty anchorages to collect copra, sell goods and drop passengers.

The Marine Department has difficulty in allocating vessels to the various district commissioners and for the major scheduled runs while also maintaining a reserve to act as relief ships when other vessels are being overhauled or repaired. By charging full commercial rates for freight the department is doing its best to discourage commercial cargoes in order to concentrate on the carriage of passengers, both official and private, but even so finds it impossible to meet the touring needs of the various government departments. This means that the remoter parts of the protectorate are visited only spasmodically, when and if ships are available. It is not always possible for a ship to keep to its schedule : it may suffer an engine breakdown or be diverted to answer an emergency call. This means that scheduled stops are sometimes visited late or even omitted altogether, which can be unpleasant for the would-be passenger waiting hopefully on a remote beach.

Considering the distances to be travelled, the rough seas and numerous reefs, accidents are comparatively rare, although vessels have piled up on rocks and been abandoned by their crew and passengers. There was one major maritime disaster in 1958 when the government vessel the *Melanesian* disappeared at sea with all hands, somewhere between Malaita and Sikaiana. As a rule, however, the worst mishap that befalls a vessel is for it to run upon a reef and have to wait there until it can be refloated at full tide.

The sailors in the government fleet are almost invariably cheerful and resourceful, whether they are on board the comparatively large *Belama* or members of the two-man crew on a 'T'-class vessel. Every vessel travels with its full complement of fishing lines extending over the side. The standard of seamanship is high, although there is a story (which seems to contain more than a grain of truth) about the bosun of one small craft who came up on deck at night to see where the ship was, only to be knocked unconscious by the branch of a tree. The ship had drifted ashore and was high and dry on a beach.

Vessels belonging to the government are maintained by the Marine Department at Tulagi in the Nggela group opposite the north coast of Guadalcanal. The slipway here can handle vessels up to 200 tons displacement. Ports used by overseas vessels are at Honiara, Tulagi, Yandina in the Russells, and in the west Gizo, Allardyce Harbour, Viru Harbour, Nila and Ringgi Cove. Shallower draft vessels in the west can use the harbour at Munda; in the east there is also an anchorage at Kirakira.

With the assistance of the government, local councils provide minor wharf facilities for local trading vessels up to 120ft in length and drawing 10ft of water. Such anchorages are to be found at about thirty places. The main port facilities exist at Honiara where there are two large concrete wharfs and four small jetties. The main deep water jetty has a concrete face 235ft long allowing vessels up to 650ft in length with draughts not in excess of 28ft to berth successfully. The main wharf for small vessels is 420ft in length and has a minimum depth alongside of 10ft. Two of the finger jetties can accommodate vessels up to 120ft long.

A number of shipping companies maintain services that call in at the Solomons. The Karlander New Guinea line provides a regular service from Australia to Honiara and New Guinea ports; a few passengers are sometimes catered for. A monthly service from Japan and Hong Kong with limited passenger accommodation is maintained by the China Navigation Company; while a monthly service from Great Britain is provided by the Bank Line, again with limited passenger accommodation. Other cargo vessels and a few oil tankers also visit Honiara and an increasing number of tourist ships are putting in for a few hours or even staying overnight. Few weeks pass without at least one overseas vessel visiting Honiara. None of the shipping lines providing passenger accommodation pretend to cater primarily for passengers, but the vessels are said by those who have travelled on them to be comfortable and unpretentious.

There are few good roads in the Solomons. Altogether there are about 140 miles of main roads, built by the Public Works Department. One road, 63 miles long, extends along the north coast of Guadalcanal on either side of Honiara. Another, 73 miles long, is on north Malaita, running from just south of Auki as far as Fouia, opposite the artificial islands of the Lau Lagoon. Both roads are drained and gravelled and 35ft wide. Constructing them has been a slow and costly business as each road includes a number of bridges over streams and rivers. Sections of both roads are frequently impassable when the rivers are in flood. In addition, there are about 325 miles of feeder and secondary roads, including private roads on plantations, forestry roads and those built by local councils.

A bus service operates in Honiara, running from White River, a few miles west of Honiara, to King George VI School and beyond, a few miles east of the town. It caters mainly for islanders coming in to work or to the market. There is also a regular bus service operating in Auki on Malaita. It usually covers only short journeys on each side of the district station, but once a day it goes as far as Fouia at the end of the main road. Buses are singledeckers; times are somewhat irregular except in Honiara where they run usually at one-hour intervals.

Four car-hire or taxi firms operate in Honiara, one of them with a desk at Honiara airport. Taxis and taxi trucks are also available for hire at Auki. The majority of taxis do not have meters and fares have not been prescribed. It is advisable to negotiate a fare with the driver before embarking on a journey. Usual rates vary between 20 and 30 cents a mile, and the most common hourly rate is about four dollars.

Great emphasis has been placed in recent years on the development of preventive medicine and on the eradication of communicable diseases such as leprosy, tuberculosis and malaria. There is an extensive rural health service, based on over a hundred clinics dispersed throughout the islands, each serving between 1,500 and 2,500 people. They are staffed by trained nurses and medical assistants, and are primarily the responsibility of local councils; at the moment the medical assistants are government-employed while the nurses are employed by the councils. They handle normal out-patient cases and the delivery of babies, and visit in the area. Cases that need special attention are referred to one of the town or district station hospitals, although bad communications are often a very real problem; here many a sick patient has to be taken to hospital over choppy seas by canoe if government shipping is not readily available.

The principal government medical institutions are the Central Hospital at Honiara, which has 159 beds, and district hospitals at Kilu'ufi near Auki on Malaita, with 112 beds; Gizo with 46, Malu'u with 36, Kirakira on San Cristobal with 64, and Buala on Santa Isabel with 36. Another hospital has recently been established at Santa Cruz. There is a training school at the Central Hospital, Honiara, for nurses and medical assistants. The Helena Goldie Hospital at Munda and the Hospital of the Epiphany at Fauabu have nurses' training schools, and there is a midwifery training school at Nafinua, all supported by the missions. In 1971 there were twenty-three registered medical officers in the protectorate.

A recent major public health project to eradicate malaria has been backed by the World Health Organisation. Trained malaria spraying teams regularly tour the islands and by the end of 1970 had dealt with all the protectorate except for the eastern district and some small outlying islands. In 1958 a successful anti-yaws

185

campaign was undertaken by WHO and UNICEF. Tuberculosis remains a problem. A central tuberculosis registry at the Central Hospital in Honiara ensures follow-up treatment for ex-patients, and BCG vaccination has been widely carried out. The incidence of new cases of leprosy has fallen in recent years. A government leprosarium twenty-three miles from Honiara is staffed by two Roman Catholic nursing sisters and is regularly visited by professional staff from the Central Hospital.

The Public Health Inspectorate, in addition to their statutory duties, have embarked with assistance from UNICEF upon a programme to introduce improved water supplies to villages. Village sanitation is still primitive, the simple pit latrine or over-water latrine being commonly used. There is, however, a growing demand for the 'pour-flush' waterseal pit latrine utilising a special type of concrete slab manufactured locally. The introduction and use of this latrine among villagers should assist considerably in the general improvement of health which has been one of the great achievements of the administration in post war years.

THE MEDIA

Communications media in the Solomons consist of a radio broadcasting service, a government news-sheet, a locally produced duplicated magazine, and a few cinemas in Honiara and at Auki and Gizo.

The Solomon Islands Broadcasting Service is run by the government although it accepts commercial advertising. It is maintained as a public service to 'reflect and unite more fully the life of the community as a whole, with an especial regard to both academic and adult education'. In this it is perhaps not outstandingly successful. It is on the air for some seven hours a day; the standards of announcing and production are not high and a great deal of the output consists of BBC transcriptions and recorded music. A daily news bulletin is prepared by the Information Service and broadcast in both English and pidgin. The use of local languages is frowned upon. On the recommendation of a visiting expert, a local Broadcasting Officer was appointed, the first Solomon Islander to become the head of a government department, and the proportion of local material as opposed to overseas programmes began to increase.

The government news-sheet is published twice a month and though it deals entirely with island affairs is similarly largely out of touch with local conditions. The size of type-face employed and the difficulty of the language used make it hard for the ordinary islander to read, and it has little influence.

Much more influential and lively is the *Kakamora Reporter*, a monthly duplicated magazine edited by a group of anonymous Solomon Islanders and published at 12 cents a copy. The *Kakamora Reporter* is irreverent, occasionally tedentious and eagerly read. Perhaps too many of the articles are pseudonymously written by disgruntled expatriate government officers, but an increasing number of Solomon Islanders are writing for it and it is becoming an accepted organ of public opinion.

The contents of the magazine vary considerably. Editorials have dealt with such matters as the pay rise granted by elected members to themselves; a defence of 'custom'; an examination of black power; and the lure of town life for young Melanesians. A popular regular series is 'Solomons Soup-Soup' in which different island types are studied as if they were specimens under a microscope: the African Exile, the Australian Cobber, the Town Drunk, the Working Wife, and many others. The readership of the *Kakamora Reporter* has increased dramatically in the year or so in which it has been going, both among islanders and among expatriates. The word *kakamora* means 'little people' and it was used as the title of his autobiography by Dr C. E. Fox, the veteran New Zealand missionary. There is a Kakamora Club in Honiara which, among other activities, sponsors a successful football team. Many of the original members of the Kakamora Club were Anglicans and there is still a feeling that the *Kakamora Reporter* is either sponsored or supported by the Melanesian Mission, though this has been firmly denied in print by the Bishop of Melanesia.

There are two commercial cinemas in Honiara and others are opening or have been opened at some of the district stations. The Point Cruz cinema in Honiara could not be described as an elegant establishment. The seats, at 75, 50 and 30 cents, are hard and when it rains the drumming of the water on the tin roof drowns the soundtrack of the film being shown. Nevertheless the film shows—three changes of movie a week—are extremely popular and the cinema is usually crowded.

Some of the government training institutions and administrative centres have 16mm projectors, and so also do some of the missions. A small film library is maintained by the Department of Education from which films may be borrowed.

POSTS AND TELECOMMUNICATIONS

An efficient system of telecommunications operates in Honiara and the district centres, but outside these centres, the only means of direct communication apart from an occasional visit from a ship, is usually the radio receiver-transmitter operated by an isolated mission station.

There is a large new General Post Office in Honiara, and district post offices at Gizo, Auki, Kirakira and Tulagi. Thirty-one postal agencies scattered about the islands handle incoming and outgoing mail and sell postage stamps. Overseas airmail is carried by Air Pacific and Trans-Australia Airlines, which make, in all, six flights a week into the Solomons. From Honiara the airmail is transferred to Solomon Islands Airways and taken to district airstrips. Postal agencies near the airstrips arrange for the further distribution of letters and parcels. A letter from the Solomons can reach the United Kingdom in three days and the United States in three to four days. Surface mail arrives mainly by Karlander Line vessels from Australia, Maritime Services vessels from New Zealand and from the United States via Australia in about six weeks.

There is a flourishing philatelic section of the Posts and Telecommunications Department. Special issues are made from time to time, commemorating such events as the South Pacific Games, and these issues are a source of revenue for the protectorate.

Since the end of World War II a telephone system has been built up within Honiara, Auki and Gizo. There are some 650 private telephones in Honiara, not counting those in government offices, about 80 at Gizo and 70 at Auki. There is an automatic telephone exchange at each district centre and in the capital and a substantial expansion of the service by underground cable is being carried out in Honiara. Three circuits are available for overseas radio telephone calls. One linked with Suva in Fiji connects with most countries in the world and is available from Monday to Saturday between 08.45 and 09.30 hours. Another links with Vila and Santo in the New Hebrides and is available from Monday to Saturday between 10.00 and 10.30 hours and from Monday to Friday between 15.00 and 15.30 hours. The third system links with Sydney in Australia, with onwards extensions to most countries, and may be used from Monday to Friday between 11.00 and 13.00, and between 14.30 and 15.00 hours.

There is a fixed rate between any two points in the Pacific region of $A4·70 for three minutes and $A1·57 for each minute thereafter. Other rates advertised by the Posts and Telecommunications Department are :

	3 Minutes $	Per Extra Minute $
Vila, Santo	3·30	1·10
Fiji	3·90	1·30
Sydney, Australia	4·50	1·50
Hong Kong (via Sydney)	8·61	2·87
United Kingdom (via Suva)	10·10	3·37
United Kingdom (via Sydney)	8·61	2·87
USA	10·80	3·60
Europe	12·00	4·00

THE SOLOMON ISLANDS

There is also an inter-island radio-telephone circuit which is open from 07.45–12.00 and 13.00–16.00, local times, with the exception of Auki, where it is continuously open. This circuit links Honiara with the district centres.

Other services provided include an aer-radio service, a cable teleprinter link, an overseas radio teleprinter service connected with Suva in Fiji and Vila in the New Hebrides, and a radio telephone service to Tarawa in the Gilbert and Ellice Islands, as well as a direct telegraph service with Rabaul in Papua–New Guinea. A radio shipping watch is operated from Honiara on a 24-hour basis and all local ships have to report their positions at stated times.

ECONOMIC EXPANSION

A number of small manufacturing firms have established themselves in and around Honiara, and in one or two other places, but none have yet achieved any great importance in the economy of the islands. Manufacturing activities include sawmilling, joinery and furniture making, shipbuilding and repair, tobacco processing and baking. Canoes and small carvings are made in some villages, and there is some basket and mat weaving. Most firms are owned by expatriates, the Malaita Development Company is one of the exceptions. 'Protected' and 'pioneer' status may be granted under existing legislation. A protected industry is in effect a monopoly, reviewed every two years, and is granted if the industry is thought to be in the public interest and unable to develop without protection. Pioneer status may be granted to new companies: concessions usually take the form of a five-year tax holiday or investment deductions allowable on capital expenditure in the range 10, 25 and 50 per cent, in addition to normal depreciation allowances.

The Solomon Islands annual report for 1969 gives a table showing the quantity and value of domestic exports over a three-year period (see opposite).

Commodity	1967 Quantity	1967 Value $	1968 Quantity	1968 Value $	1969 Quantity	1969 Value $
Copra (tons)	24,434	3,628,731	17,217	3,625,384	24,463	3,470,665
Timber (cuft)	2,843,238	1,079,081	4,438,795	1,412,159	7,335,169	2,474,813
Cocoa (tons)	59	22,163	118	52,288	85	50,909
Marine shell (cwt)	8,331	55,393	6,640	44,040	12,441	82,423
Scrap metal (tons)	179	57,117	233	63,110	252	33,073
Crocodile skins	—	6,055	—	4,081	—	5,839
Gold (troy oz)	672	17,252	654	17,741·	413	11,521
Navy biscuits (lb)	220,000	29,260	200,000	26,600	281,200	37,277
Manufactured tobacco (lb)	2,410	3,133	15,678	16,193	46,908	49,132
Other exports	—	46,135	—	38,376	—	91,146
Total		4,911,927		5,299,972		6,306,798

The principal destinations of domestic exports over this three-year period were :

	1967 per cent	1968 per cent	1969 per cent
Britain	42·8	55·5	44·1
Japan	40·0	24·8	40·2
Australia	15·1	17·0	13·0
Other countries	2·1	2·7	2·7
Total	100·0	100·0	100·0

Imported goods are distributed through several large importers, small storekeepers, commission agents and the missions. There are trading stores, many Chinese-owned, at Honiara, Gizo, Auki and Tulagi, and small stores and co-operatives run by Solomon Islanders, and in some cases Chinese or Europeans, exist throughout the group. The principal countries from which goods were imported over a recent five-year period were :

	1965 per cent	1966 per cent	1967 per cent	1968 per cent	1969 per cent
Australia	44·1	40·0	44·6	45·0	43·8
Britain	25·0	15·8	20·0	19·6	18·7
Hong Kong	5·3	5·3	5·4	4·3	3·9
Japan	4·1	6·4	5·1	4·8	6·1
Singapore	—	0·7	2·8	5·6	4·0
USA	5·5	13·6	10·3	9·4	6·3
Others	16·0	18·2	11·8	11·3	17·2
Total	100·0	100·0	100·0	100·0	100·0

The market for imports is relatively small. Whereas a few expatriate families with high incomes demand a wide range of sophisticated goods but not in considerable bulk, the larger indigenous population requires, or is able to afford, a much narrower range of basic goods. It must also be remembered that the total work force in the Solomons is not high in relation to the population. In 1969 the annual report summarised it as follows :

192

Employed in Agriculture :	2,325
Forestry :	928
Government :	3,895
Local Government :	393
All other employment :	5,536

Total   13,077

Although more and more islanders are seeking paid employment in order to achieve a higher standard of living, the amount of cash available is not large and there would seem to be limited room for expansion of commercial ventures catering solely or mainly for the local market. Expansion seems possible in areas involving timber, mineral ore refining and some agricultural exports, but in all these concerns the expenditure of considerable capital would be necessary; also, by developing country standards, wage rates in the Solomons are quite high and, though there is usually a ready supply of unskilled labour, skilled islanders are in short supply. The basic wage of an unskilled labourer, newly engaged, is one dollar a day paid monthly for a five-day week. According to skill and experience long-serving labourers and artisans can obtain up to three dollars a day. Employers are required to provide accommodation, water, sanitary arrangements and medical care for all workers who cannot return to their homes after work.

Timber is exported by a number of commercial firms, most of it going to Japan, some to Australia. Lever's Pacific Timbers at Kolombangara in the west exports about 4 million cubic feet a year; Kalena Timbers at Viru Harbour, also in the west, a little over 1 million; on Santa Isabel the Allardyce Lumber Company produces almost 1½ million annually and a Japanese firm operating in the Shortlands about 700,00 cubic feet. It is estimated that a great deal more timber could be produced in the Solomons, but one of the major problems in this area is the matter of obtaining land. Islanders are fiercely jealous of their traditional land rights and are often reluctant to allow their

M

land to be surveyed or examined. This is a matter exercising both the Department of Lands and Surveys and the Forestry Department in the consideration of large-scale development in agriculture, forestry and mining. Customary land can only be sold or leased to the government; it cannot be alienated to non-Solomon Islanders.

One of the government's main economic hopes is that the bauxite deposits on the Polynesian island of Rennell will one day bring in a substantial annual revenue. It is thought that deposits are sufficient to yield 1½ million tons a year for about twelve years. The Japanese Mitsui Company has been granted prospecting rights and mining is expected to begin in 1974. If all goes well the government's annual income may be in the region of A\$350,000, while the owners of the land should share about A\$18,000 a year.

Tourism is only a minor industry at the moment and is based almost entirely on Honiara. There certainly seems to be a growth potential. Travel through and within the Pacific area is expected to increase by 500 per cent over the next ten years, and the Solomons will share in the increasing prosperity. There is an official Solomon Islands Tourist Authority in Honiara, and two sizeable travel agencies which arrange local tours of Honiara, Guadalcanal and some of the adjacent islands.

8   HONIARA HOLIDAYS

Honiara, the capital, is a small, pleasant and usually sun-drenched town on the Guadalcanal plain. It has a compact harbour, one main street and is overlooked by a series of ridges which climb to the mountain ranges of the interior. About 12,000 people live in the town which is also the business and administrative centre of the protectorate.

Most visitors to the Solomons spend the greater part of their stay in Honiara, landing at Honiara airport just a few miles from the town when they fly in from Fiji, the New Hebrides or Papua–New Guinea. It is possible to fly from Honiara to other islands, and even to return the same day, but very few visitors take advantage of this opportunity. In fact most tourists do not stay long in the Solomons but come to the islands on short pack-age-tours, often in the course of a conducted tour of the South Pacific. In 1970, 1,739 holiday-makers came to the islands, the majority staying for less than a week.

Honiara is a charming modern South Seas town, relatively un-spoiled by Pacific islands standards. There are no beggars or touts, little if any commercialisation, and tipping in hotels and restuarants is frowned upon as it is regarded as lowering the dignity of those serving.

There are at present three hotels in Honiara. None of them would ever be confused with the Hilton but all are clean, comfortable and amiably staffed and run. The largest is the Hotel Mendana. This is situated in the centre of the town on the main street and has its own beach. It is fully licensed and all rooms are air-conditioned with showers, toilets, telephones and refrigerators. All members of the staff speak English and the waiters, in white shirts and orange lap laps, must be among the most friendly and charming in the world. The price of rooms, including breakfast, at present ranges from $A9 to A$12 per person per room. This is not cheap, although neither is it particularly expensive by South Pacific standards. The hotel is often full and it is advisable to book rooms well in advance.

The Honiara Hotel is a mile from the centre of the town on the road to Honiara airport. This is smaller than the Mendana and has no sea view, although there is a swimming pool. Rooms are comfortable, carpeted and air-conditioned. Rates, including breakfast, run from $A10 to $A12 per person per room. Both Chinese and European food is served, and this hotel also is fully licensed.

In a quiet central area is Blum's Hometel, which provides motel-type accommodation. All rooms are self-contained, with ceiling fans, cooking facilities and refrigerators. A restaurant on the premises, the Hibiscus Room, provides simple meals and snacks. Current rates, for accommodation only, vary from $A4·50 per person in twin rooms to $A6 per person in single occupancy.

Twenty-eight miles by road from Honiara, on the way to the western extremity of the north coast of Guadalcanal, is the tourist resort of Tambea. This consists of a number of bungalows constructed in Melanesian style, offering single or double accommodation. Although the bungalows are of the traditional leaf material the proprietors offer visitors the best of both worlds as each bungalow has its own shower, toilet and hot and cold water. A 24-hour service is provided and there are two bars, a barbecue area and beer gardens. There is a pleasant beach and boats and canoes may be hired. A variety of local entertainment is offered, including Melanesian dances and visits to a nearby village. Rates range from $A10 for a single room to $A14 for double accommodation. Tambea Village Resort is an attractive and interesting spot, but a long way from Honiara. A car must be hired in order to visit the capital. There is a great deal of interest in the immediate vicinity, however; the site was a former pagan place of sacrifice and contains four Christian graves whose traditional task it is to keep the local spirit devil well under ground.

Yet another resort on Guadalcanal is Tavanipupu Island in Marau Sound, sixty-five miles from Honiara, and it can be reached by Solomon Islands Airways or, more laboriously, by sea. There are two fully-equipped and attractive cottages, each accommodating four people, and extra guests may be housed in an annexe. This is definitely a resort for those wishing to see the real Solomons and is not recommended for travellers in search of a sophisticated holiday. Swimming, fishing and shelling are the main recreations available and scuba gear may be hired. Provisions can be delivered by arrangement but guests have to do their own cooking. Rates are $A80 per week per cottage. This includes the use of a boat with an outboard motor, but fuel is extra. The airstrip is on the mainland opposite the island, and there is an attractive Roman Catholic mission station close at hand.

AROUND THE TOWN

Those holiday-makers who decide to remain in Honiara will usually find enough to occupy them. They must be prepared for a hot and humid climate and a leisurely pace to life.

Normal wear for men is shorts and a sports shirt, and for women light summer dresses. The older islanders do not like to see women in shorts, although girls in the capital took to the mini-skirt with alacrity. An umbrella is useful, both for keeping off the sun and in case of a sudden shower. Raincoats are too hot.

The people of Honiara are genuinely friendly. No visitor should hesitate to ask for directions or assistance, both will readily be forthcoming. The official line of the local tourist agency is that there is no tipping in the Solomons and this is generally adhered to. A practice which is very much deplored is that of tossing coins to local children. This could encourage begging, as it has in other island groups, and it emphatically is not a custom of the dignified Solomon Islanders.

There is one main shopping centre running through the town, with shops and stores on both sides. The largest shop is the British Solomons Trading Company, and there are several supermarkets. The ubiquitous Chinese stores sell everything under the sun, but most of these are found in Chinatown, a winding thoroughfare just outside the town over the Matanikau bridge. A modified form of duty-free shopping is possible at five shops in Honiara: the British Solomons Trading Company, H. M. Long Radio Sales, Melanchine Shipping and Forwarding Agency, Mendana Electrics, and Quan Hong and Co, Ltd. The range of duty-free goods includes transistor radios, record players, tape recorders, cameras, watches, pearls, binoculars, jewellery and liquor. Carvings may be bought in many local shops, but carvers themselves often visit the hotels with their work. It is sometimes possible to bargain with an islander but when a carver has once put a price on his goods he seldom likes to haggle. A notable feature of Honiara is the wide range of prices asked for identical goods in different shops, and prospective purchasers would do well to visit several stores before buying anything; they should also look carefully at ebony —it could be an ordinary wood blackened with shoe polish.

Most shops open from 8am to 12.30pm and 2 to 5pm, Monday to Friday; and 8am to 12.30pm on Saturday. Some Chinese stores stay open until late into the evening. Office hours vary but most government departments open from 7.30am until noon and from 1pm until 4 or 4.30. Banks—the Commonwealth Bank and the Australian and New Zealand Bank—are open from 9 to 11.30am and 1.30 to 3pm Monday to Friday with an extra hour on Friday afternoons when they close at 4pm. The General Post Office is open from 8am till noon and from 1pm to 5pm, Monday to Friday; and on Saturday morning from 8 to 11am.

Medical, dental and pharmaceutical services are available at

198

the Central Hospital, Honiara. Some pharmaceutical supplies are also available in shops. There is a ladies' hairdressing salon in the town.

In the centre of the town is a museum which displays traditional artifacts, war relics and geological exhibits as well as butterfly and shell collections, and where handicrafts are available for purchase. The Botanical Gardens and Herbarium are only a short distance out, but it is recommended that they be visited towards the end of the afternoon when it is comparatively cool.

Holiday-makers are always most welcome at the churches in the capital—Anglican, Roman Catholic, United (Methodist), South Sea Evangelical, Seventh Day Adventist and Baha'i Community—and should be prepared for the sight, unusual in Europe, of full churches at most services. They are advised to check with the minister that the service they wish to attend is in fact to be conducted in English. As a general rule the services are in pidgin or island dialect on Sunday mornings, but in English in the evenings.

Tennis, swimming and bowls are available at the Guadalcanal Club, sailing at the Point Cruz Yacht Club, and there is a golf club just outside the town. Honorary membership of all clubs is usually available. Visitors are warned not to swim in the sea or in river mouths as there is a very real danger from sharks. Spectator sports include Rugby and Association Football. The Rugby season is from November till April and Association Football is played between April and October. There are local league games on some evenings and on Saturday afternoons; the standard is not yet high but the Solomon Islands Rugby Football XV won a bronze medal at the South Pacific Games in 1969, coming in third to the Pacific giants of Fiji and Tonga. There are also occasional well-supported local amateur boxing tournaments, again notable more for their enthusiasm than for the degree of skill displayed. Some cricket is played but mostly between teams comprising a large proportion of expatriate players.

199

The small and attractive High Court is sure to be pointed out. Here the Chief Justice of the High Court of the Western Pacific presides. There is a magistrates' court, with both civil and criminal jurisdiction—magistrates in the protectorate are not professionally qualified and the High Court has the power to reverse decisions.

Close to the High Court building is the police station. The Solomons police force is not a large one, consisting of 12 gazetted officers, an inspectorate of 11 and 296 officers and men deployed throughout the four districts. Its headquarters is on the outskirts of Honiara and has a police training school attached to it. Crime rate in the Solomons is about twenty per thousand of the population and crimes are usually minor ones; the people generally are tolerant and law-abiding. In the capital the relatively high cost of living and the shortage of work are probably responsible for the occasional cases of housebreaking, while a few brawls after pay-day drinking sessions also result in court cases.

It will be seen that those expatriates who live in and around Honiara, government officers and their families, do so in considerable comfort in their modern detached houses, many of them with large gardens and swimming pools. Rents are subsidised and the average family employs several servants. Houseboys receive anything between 20 and 35 dollars a month and free accommodation, usually a small house attached to the main building but sometimes a separate dwelling. Unskilled gardeners and labourers working as servants receive between 15 and 20 dollars a month. Such wages are not really adequate and men with large families find great difficulty in making ends meet. The same can be said of unskilled labourers generally and also of the lower-paid government clerical officers living in the several housing estates behind the town or in the dormitories and houses for bachelors in the labour lines just outside Honiara. It was recently decided that the minimum wage for labourers should be 10 cents an hour or $A19·80 a month, but this was greeted with a great deal of derision as being totally unrealistic.

200

Conditions are worsened by the fact that many people from the districts come in to Honiara to stay with relations working there. By custom a worker must house and feed his relatives for as long as they wish to stay. For a man already straining to keep himself and his family this can be an almost intolerable burden. A further complication lies in the increasing number of young men with standard 7 education who have completed a senior primary school course but are debarred from entering government service because of the insistence of at least two years of secondary education for government workers. These young men often do not want to go back to their villages so they come into the capital. Some find work as labourers but the majority merely live with relations and are beginning to present a considerable social problem.

As most Solomon Isanders in the capital have little money to spare their recreations are few and simple. A small community centre is not greatly patronised. Some of them own canoes and go fishing off the coast of Guadalcanal. On Saturdays the local football matches attract large crowds and round pay day the cinema and the beer garden of the Hotel Mendana are popular places. The Honiara Club caters mainly for Solomon Islanders, particularly those in the middle-income brackets. The three other clubs in or near Honiara—the Guadalcanal Club, the Point Cruz Yacht Club and the Golf Club—operate no colour bar as such but the high cost of subscriptions ($A24 a year for the Guadalcanal Club) effectively bar all but the most highly paid islanders from membership. At the moment Honiara is definitely a town of the haves and have-nots.

OFF TO OTHER PLACES

Apart from the organised conducted tours laid on by the travel firms (*see* p 194) it is possible to hire a car and make some interesting journeys around the capital. A self-drive hired car cost about $A12 a day, so such excursions are not cheap. Any fare for a taxi journey should be negotiated before the trip is made: it is a regrettable fact that in a town where tourists are made particularly welcome one or two taxi drivers are giving the rest a bad name by over-charging. When in doubt about a fare, it is advisable to check in advance at the travel agency or the Solomon Islands Tourist Authority office. A pamphlet of recognised drives and walks around Honiara is available from the travel agencies, Tourist Authority or Department of Information. One of the drives takes in the Matanikau river area, the location of some of the fiercest fighting of the Guadalcanal campaign. From the road eastwards out of Chinatown, the route follows the river along what used to be known as the Marine Trail, built by the Americans during the war to supply their fighting troops. On returning to the main road and heading east again the visitor can stop at the attractively designed Anglican Cathedral of St Barnabas before turning right and driving up to Kola'a Ridge to get a series of fine views along the coast. Back on the main coastal road to Kukum there is a fishing village of some interest and also the Technical Institute, the Marine Training School and, a little farther along, King George VI School. Beyond this a bridge across the Lunga river takes the car past Lever's Lunga Plantation and Henderson Field to the end of the notorious Bloody Ridge, where the Americans defended the airfield so grimly. The next river is the Ilu, known mistakenly during the war as the Tenaru, and the site of a number of bloody encounters. The undergrowth on the side of the road on the far side of the bridge is called Hell's Point and is the dumping ground of thousands of tons of high explosives. This area is dangerous and should not be entered.

Four miles from Henderson Field the road crosses Dodo Creek and reaches Tenaru, where there is a sawmill and several small stores. The beach here is known as Red Beach, where the American marines came ashore on 7 August 1942. The road continues over the grasslands of Okea, where Guadalcanal Plains Ltd have their ricefields and mill, crosses the Nalimbu river and runs along part of the abandoned Koli airstrip before crossing the Matepona river on a modern high-level bridge.

After passing Tetere Leprosarium on the left, a branch road leads down to Tetere beach, from which there is a very good view of Tatuve mountain. A few minutes' walk along the beach to the right leads to a memorial to five Austrian scientists who were massacred in 1896 when attempting to climb the sacred mountain. The main road leads to the Balasuna river, 24 miles from Honiara, where a high-level bridge carries the road over to the grasslands of Berande. The return trip to Honiara may be made along this road in less than an hour if no detours are taken.

An equally interesting car journey may be made along the road leading westwards out of the capital. Before leaving the town, however, one can turn left past St John's School and visit the Herbarium where specimens of local flora are catalogued and stored. It stands in a pleasantly wooded and grassed valley, through which a little stream runs down a course of rock pools. The lily pond and its specimens at the foot of a giant ivory-nut palm are especially attractive.

Return to the main road and continue westwards past the police headquarters to White River, a Gilbertese settlement where some of the 2,000 resettled Gilbert and Ellice Islanders live. Farther along, and about 3 miles from the town, is the village of Kakambona where the Japanese had their field headquarters during the war.

The road continues along the coast for some 20 miles to Cape Esperance at the north-west extremity of Guadalcanal, passing through plantations and villages and across numerous rivers. In the rainy season care should be taken before leaving the capital to find out whether or not these rivers are in flood, as they can be dangerous. At Visale, 25 miles from Honiara, is a Roman Catholic mission station, with its very fine church standing just back from the road. Past Visale are many more villages and also the tourist resort village of Tambea. The road eventually ends

203

at Lambi, 35 miles from Honiara, but plans are in hand to extend it. The return journey to Honiara must be made by the same route.

For the adventurous it is perfectly possible to organise one's own tours and trips further afield by negotiating with the owners of taxis and canoes, but in order to see as much as possible without undue wear and tear the services of one of the local travel agencies should be enlisted. Both Guadalcanal Travel Service and Hunts of the Pacific organise group and individual tours and will provide details, which are also obtainable from the Solomon Islands Tourist Authority in Honiara.

Among the day and half-day trips arranged are conducted tours of the Guadalcanal battlefields, including a meeting with Jacob Vouza, the Solomons' war hero; a trip by boat along the coast to visit the scene of various sea battles; tours of Melanesian villages; skin-diving and shelling expeditions; a canoe-trip up the Matanikau river; a trip by aeroplane over Guadalcanal, and visits to other islands which should be included in the itinerary if at all possible. A day tour to the volcanic island of Savo takes in both the hot springs and the megapode bird sanctuary, while an aeroplane flight across Guadalcanal to Marau Sound or to Avu Avu transports visitors into genuine 'bush' country. A sea trip to Tulagi, scene of some of the fiercest fighting of the war, is also offered.

Perhaps the most interesting trip of all is the one to the artificial island of Laulasi in the Langa Langa Lagoon, off Malaita's south-eastern coast. This trip occupies the greater part of a day and is undertaken by aircraft, motor vehicle and large canoe. The aircraft leaves from Henderson Field for Auki, the district station of Malaita, passing over Tulagi, the former capital, en route. At Gwaunaru'u airstrip just outside Auki a brief tour of the local village is arranged and then a motor vehicle is provided for the journey to Auki, some six miles away. Auki itself is a very attractive South Sea town with a few government offices, a number of Chinese stores and traditional houses. From the small

204

wharf, which is usually very busy, a large canoe continues the tour to Laulasi, past Auki island to the beautiful Langa Langa Lagoon. The run takes about an hour, then the canoe ties up at Laulasi wharf and visitors are shown round. They see the traditional manufacture of shell money and—though the island is now Christian—something of the shark worship that still has a number of adherents among the older people. Tours of the sacred places are arranged, but visitors must not enter any of them without permission of the guides. Tourists are also requested not to wear clothing that is predominantly red or black in colour as both these colours are tabu, forbidden by custom, as it is believed that they can destroy ability to find good fishing grounds.

The origins of Laulasi and the reasons for its being built in the first place are uncertain. (*See* p 56). A Laulasi legend claims that this particular island was built because the people wanted to be near a beautiful woman who first taught them the art of making shell money. Certainly Laulasi is the only island in the area where this art is still practised. Other artificial islands in the lagoon, impressed by the number of visitors received by Laulasi, have intimated that they also would like to receive tourists.

Visitors to the Solomons able to afford the time to stay elsewhere may also fly to the western district centre of Gizo, where there is an hotel. Also in the west is the holiday cottage of Liapari, near Barakoma airstrip. This is a fully furnished cottage situated on a beautiful bay. Electricity is laid on and so is running water and a refrigerator. Linen and cutlery are provided. The cottage can accommodate four and is close to a trading store. A dinghy and outboard motor are provided free of charge while a speedboat and water skiing kit can be hired. Rates for accommodation are $A50 a week or $A10 a day.

BIBLIOGRAPHY

CHAPTER 1

ALLEN, C. H. *Customary Land Tenure in the British Solomon Islands Protectorate.* Honiara BSIP, 1957

BALLANTYNE, A. O. *Report on the Soil Survey of Guadalcanal Plain and other Areas of the British Solomon Islands Protectorate.* Honiara BSIP, 1961

GROVER, J. C. (ed). *The British Solomon Islands Geological Record,* vol 1, 1953–1956, vol 2, 1957–1958, vol 3, 1959–1962

GUPPY, H. B. *The Solomon Islands: Their Geology, General Features and Suitability for Colonization.* London, 1887

GUPPY, H. B. *The Solomon Islands and their Natives.* London, 1887

MAYRE, E. *Birds of the Southwest Pacific.* London, 1945

PLEYDELL, G. J. *Timbers of the British Solomon Islands.* Levers Pacific Timbers Ltd, 1970

WALKER, F. S. *The Forests of the British Solomon Islands Protectorate.* South Pacific Commission, Noumea, 1962

WHITMORE, T. C. *Guide to the Forests of the British Solomon Islands.* Oxford, 1966

Annual Reports of the British Solomon Islands Protectorate
Annual Reports of the Department of Forestry
Annual Reports of the Department of Geological Survey
Geology, Mineral Deposits and Prospects of Mining Development in the Solomons, 1955. Memoir no 1 of the Geological Survey
Information leaflets issued by the BSIP Department of Information :
  The British Solomon Islands
  Guadalcanal
  Polynesian Islands of the Solomons
  Malaita
  Savo

BIBLIOGRAPHY

CHAPTER 2

BELSHAW, C. S. *Changing Melanesia*. Oxford, 1954
BLACKWOOD, B. *Both Sides of the Buka Passage*. Oxford, 1935
COCHRANE, G. *Big Men and Cargo Cults*. Oxford, 1970
COCHRANE, G. 'Racialism in the Pacific', *Oceania*, vol 40, no 1, Sept 1969
CODRINGTON, R. H. *The Melanesians*. Oxford, 1891 (reprinted 1969)
CRANSTONE, B. A. L. *Melanesia: A Short Ethnography*. London, 1961
DAVENPORT, W. 'Notes on Santa Cruz Voyaging', *Journal of the Polynesian Society*, vol 73, no 2, June 1964
DAVENPORT, W. 'Red Feather Money', *Scientific American*, vol 206, no 3, March 1962
ELKIN, A. P. *Social Anthropology in Melanesia*. London, 1953
FIRTH, R. *We, the Tikopia*. London, 1936
FREEMAN, J. D. and GEDDES, W. R. *Anthropology in the South Seas*. Auckland, 1959
FOX, C. E. *The Threshold of the Pacific*. London, 1924
HOGBIN, H. I. *A Guadalcanal Society*. New York, 1965
HOGBIN, H. I. 'Coconuts and Coral Islands', *National Geographic Magazine*. March 1934
IVENS, W. G. *Melanesians of the South-Eastern Solomons*. London, 1927
IVENS, W. G. *The Island Builders of the Pacific*. London, 1930
KEESING, F. *The South Seas in the Modern World*. London, 1942
MALINOWSKI, B. *Argonauts of the Western Pacific*. New York, 1922
OLIVER, D. L. *A Solomon Island Society*. Cambridge, Mass, 1955
RIVERS, W. H. R. *The History of Melanesian Society*. Cambridge, 1914
SCHEFFLER, H. *Choiseul Island Social Structure*. Los Angeles, 1965
WHEELER, C. G. *Mono-Alu Folklore*. London, 1926

The Journal of the Polynesian Society. Wellington, New Zealand.
Mankind: Journal of the Anthropological Society of Australia. Sydney
Oceania. University of Sydney, New South Wales

CHAPTER 3

AMHERST, LORD, and THOMSON, BASIL. *The Discovery of the Solomon Islands by Alvaro de Mendana in 1568* (2 vols) Hakluyt Society. London, 1901
BEAGLEHOLE, J. C. *The Exploration of the Pacific*. London, 1934
BUCK, P. *Explorers of the Pacific*. Honolulu, 1953
BURNEY, J. *A Chronological History of the Voyages and Discoveries in the South Seas, or Pacific Ocean* (5 vols). London, 1803–17
CALLENDAR, J. *Terra Australis Cognita: or, Voyages to the Terra Australis, or Southern Hemisphere, during the 16th, 17th and 18th Centuries* (3 vols). Edinburgh, 1766–68
DALRYMPLE, A. *An Historical Collection of the Several Voyages and Discoveries in the South Pacific Ocean* (2 vols). London, 1770–71
FOX, C. E. *The Story of the Solomons*. Honiara, 1967
HAWKESWORTH, J. *An Account of the Voyages . . . by Captain Byron, Captain Wallis, Captain Carteret, and Captain Cook . . .* (3 vols). London, 1773
JACK-HINTON, C. *The Search for the Islands of Solomon 1567–1838*. Oxford, 1969
MARKHAM, SIR C. *The Voyages of Pedro Fernandez de Quiros, 1595–1606* (2 vols). Hakluyt Society, London, 1904
MAUDE, H. E. *Of Islands and Men*. Oxford, 1968
OLIVER, D. *The Pacific Islands*. Cambridge, Mass, 1951
PHILLIP, A. *The Voyage of Governor Phillip to Botany Bay . . . to which are added the Journals of Lieuts Shortland, Watts, Ball, and Capt Marshall, with an Account of their Discoveries*. London, 1789
SHARP, A. *The Discovery of the Pacific Islands*. Oxford, 1960
WROTH, L. C. *The Early Cartography of the Pacific*. New York, 1944

CHAPTER 4

ARMSTRONG, E. S. *The History of the Melanesian Mission*. London, 1900
BELSHAW, C. S. *Island Administration in the South-West Pacific*. Oxford, 1950

BIBLIOGRAPHY

BRENCHLEY, J. L. *Jottings during the Cruise of HMS 'Curaçoa' among the South Seas Islands in 1865.* London, 1873

BURTT, J. *Reminiscences re George Augustus Selwyn DD.* London, 1907

CHEESMAN, E. *Backwaters of the Savage South Seas.* London, 1929

CHURCHWARD, W. B. *Blackbirding in the South Pacific.* London, 1888

COOTE, W. *The Western Pacific 1875–1881.* London, 1883

DAKIN, W. S. *Whaleman Adventurers.* Sydney, 1934

DILLON, P. *Narrative of a Voyage in the South Seas.* London, 1829

DUNBABIN, T. *Slavers of the South Seas.* Sydney, 1935

EVANS, J. H. *Churchman Militant: George Augustus Selwyn.* Wellington, 1964

FOX, C. E. *Lord of the Southern Isles.* London, 1958

FOX, C. E. *Kakamora.* London, 1962

KNIBBS, S. *The Savage Solomons as they Were and Are.* London, 1929

ROMILLY, H. H. *Letters from the Western Pacific and Mashonoland, 1878–1891.* London, 1893

SCARR, D. *Fragments of Empire.* Canberra, 1967

WOODFORD, C. M. *A Naturalist Among the Headhunters.* London, 1890

YONGE, C. M. *Life of John Coleridge Patteson.* London, 1894

CHAPTER 5

BERNATZIK, H. *Sudsee.* London, 1935

C.O.I. *Among Those Present.* London, 1946

COLLINSON, C. W. *Life and Laughter 'Midst the Cannibals.* London (undated)

COLWELL, J. (ed) *A Century in the Pacific.* Sydney, 1914

DONOVAN, R. J. *PT 109: John F. Kennedy in World War II.* New York, 1961

FELDT, E. *The Coast Watchers.* Sydney, 1946

FOWLER, W. *This Island is Mine.* London, 1959

HEALY, A. M. *Administration in the British Solomon Islands Journal of Administration Overseas.*

HORTON, D. C. *The Happy Isles.* London, 1965

HORTON, D. C. *Fire Over the Islands.* Wellington, 1971

210

BIBLIOGRAPHY

JOHNSON, O. *Bride in the Solomons.* London, 1946
LAMBERT, S. M. *A Doctor in Paradise.* London, 1941
MACQUARRIE, H. *Vouza and the Solomon Islands.* London, 1945
MILLER, J. *Guadalcanal: the First Offensive.* Washington, 1949
MYTINGER, C. *Headhunting in the Solomon Islands.* London, 1943
PHILLIPS, J. S. *Coconut Quest.* London, 1940
RENTZ, J. N. *Marines in the Central Solomons.* Washington, 1952
STRUBEN, R. *Coral and the Colour of Gold.* London, 1961
ZIMMERMAN, J. L. *The Guadalcanal Campaign.* Washington, 1949

CHAPTER 6

ALLEN, C. H. 'The Marching Rule', *Corona*, vol 3, no 3, 1951
BOGESI, G. 'Santa Isabel', *Oceania*, vol 18, 1948
DAVENPORT, W. and COKER, G. 'The Moro Movement of Guadal-
canal, British Solomon Islands Protectorate', *Journal of the Poly-
nesian Society*, vol 76, June 1967
HEALY, A. M. *Administration in the British Solomon Islands,
Journal of Administration Overseas*, mid-sixties
HOGBIN, H. I. 'Notes and Instructions to Native Administrations
in the Solomon Islands', *Oceania*, vol 16, 1945
LAWRENCE, P. *Road Belong Cargo.* Manchester, 1964
MAIR, L. P. 'The Pursuit of the Millennium in Melanesia', *British
Journal of Sociology*, vol 9, 1958
TEDDER, J. L. O. 'The Solomon Islands—an Emerging Cash
Economy', *Australian Geographical Studies*, vol 4, no 1, April
1966
TEDDER, J. L. O. 'Honiara', *South Pacific Bulletin*, vol 16, no 1,
1966
WORSLEY, P. *The Trumpet Shall Sound.* MacGibbon & Kee, 1957

Annual Report, BSIP. 1950–70
Pacific Islands Monthly

CHAPTER 7

Annual Department Reports, BSIP. Honiara, 1950–70
Conditions and Cost of Living in the Protectorate, 1968. Honiara

BIBLIOGRAPHY

Educational Policy (White Paper). Honiara, 1967
Local Councils (White Paper). Honiara, 1962
Western Pacific Commission—Fifth Development Plan 1968–1970.
Honiara, 1970
Western Pacific High Commission—Sixth Development Plan 1971–1974. Honiara, 1971

CHAPTER 8

CORNER, E. S. H. (ed) *A Discussion on the Results of the Royal Society Expedition to the British Solomon Islands Protectorate, 1965.* London, 1969
GROVER, J. (ed) *Transactions of the British Solomon Islands Society.* Honiara
SCOTT, R. J. *Report on the Prospects for the Tourist Industry in the British Solomon Islands Protectorate.* Honiara, 1968

Publications of the British Solomon Islands Tourist Authority

ACKNOWLEDGEMENTS

So many Solomon Islanders have showed me kindness and hospitality during the years I have spent touring the islands that it is extremely difficult to single out those who were particularly generous with their time and knowledge. I would, however, like to express my gratitude to Jimmy and Adela Kenekene of Kalaka on Savo; Peter Noel Orudiana of the Lau Lagoon; Markson Koroa of Tikopia; and Selena Tale of the Marovo Lagoon. None of my touring would have been possible without the assistance of my travelling companion, Joanna Rua of East Malaita. Among those who allowed me to live and travel with them were the Reverend and Mrs Burley Mesepitu of Simbo; the Reverend and Mrs Lorima Uluiqaravau of Gizo; the Reverend and Mrs Luke Pitu of Marovo; and the Reverend and Mrs Igan Lokekale of Aola. John Steward and his family of Verahue showed me great kindness when I was stranded at his village on one occasion, and Medical Assistant Philemon Pitakaka was equally kind when I was left without transport on Santa Isabel. My travelling in the Western Solomons was arranged with great efficiency by Bishop Leslie Boseto of the United Church. Among my travelling companions who accepted a European woman on their trips with charm and courtesy were Dr Francis Kikolo and Assistant Education Officer Michael Sivainao. These, of course were only a few out of many hundreds of islanders who showed such kindness to me and to my children on our travels.

For reminiscences of the past I am indebted to Timothy Lopiga of Asimae for details of his life on the Queensland sugar plantations at the turn of the century, and for information about the

213

ACKNOWLEDGEMENTS

death of District Officer Bell on Malaita. Father Joseph of Ruavatu was also a mine of information about life in the Solomons in the early days of the twentieth century, as was the doyen of Pacific islands missionaries, Dr Charles Fox. D. C. Horton supplied much valuable information about government administration in the Solomons immediately before World War II and about the exploits of the coastwatchers during the war. Islanders Bill Bennett and Jacob Vouza, both themselves decorated for gallantry, also provided many reminiscences about the war on Guadalcanal and in the western Solomons.

Among the Europeans living in the Solomons, the missionaries of all faiths living and working among the people provided much information about the islands.

I have stayed and learned much at the mission stations of Tangarare, Vonunu, Munda, Afio, Sasamunga and Auki.

INDEX

215

INDEX